TROOP LEADER
planner

IF FOUND, PLEASE RETURN TO :

....

....

....

WILD simplicity

Paper Co. x Est. 2019

TABLE OF CONTENTS

TROOP INFORMATION

4   TROOP LEADER & VOLUNTEER CONTACT INFORMATION

9   SERVICE UNIT INFORMATION & CONTACTS

10   COUNCIL INFORMATION & CONTACTS

11   TROOP ROSTER

21   TROOP BIRTHDAYS

CALENDARS

22   UNDATED MONTHLY CALENDARS

PLANNERS & TRACKERS

36   MEETING PLANNERS

76   BADGE ACTIVITY PLANNERS

106   FLEXIBLE TRACKERS

FINANCES

116   TROOP DUES & BUDGET PLANNER

118   TROOP FINANCES

120   TROOP LEADER TAX-DEDUCTIBLE EXPENSES

121   TROOP LEADER TAX-DEDUCTIBLE MILEAGE

COOKIE SALES

122   COOKIE BOOTH PLANNER

124   COOKIE BOOTH SALES TRACKERS

VOLUNTEER LOGS

134   VOLUNTEER SIGN-UP SHEETS

140   SNACK SIGN-UP SHEETS

142   VOLUNTEER DRIVER LOGS

MISCELLANEOUS

147   LISTS & NOTES

TROOP LEADER & VOLUNTEER CONTACT INFORMATION

NAME: ☐ BACKGROUND CHECK

TROOP LEADER PHONE: (......)................... EMAIL: ....

NOTES:

NAME: ☐ BACKGROUND CHECK

TROOP LEADER PHONE: (......)................... EMAIL: ....

NOTES:

NAME: ☐ BACKGROUND CHECK

VOLUNTEER TROOP MEMBER:...........................'S ☐ PARENT/GUARDIAN ☐ GRANDPARENT ☐ SIBLING ☐ OTHER:...............

TROOP ROLE(S): ☐ TREASURER ☐ COOKIE MANAGER ☐ FALL PRODUCT MANAGER ☐ CHAPERONE ☐ DRIVER ☐ GENERAL HELPER ☐ OTHER:...............

PHONE: (......)........... EMAIL:................. SPECIAL SKILLS:...............

NOTES:

NAME: ☐ BACKGROUND CHECK

VOLUNTEER TROOP MEMBER:...........................'S ☐ PARENT/GUARDIAN ☐ GRANDPARENT ☐ SIBLING ☐ OTHER:...............

TROOP ROLE(S): ☐ TREASURER ☐ COOKIE MANAGER ☐ FALL PRODUCT MANAGER ☐ CHAPERONE ☐ DRIVER ☐ GENERAL HELPER ☐ OTHER:...............

PHONE: (......)........... EMAIL:................. SPECIAL SKILLS:...............

NOTES:

NAME: ☐ BACKGROUND CHECK

VOLUNTEER TROOP MEMBER:...........................'S ☐ PARENT/GUARDIAN ☐ GRANDPARENT ☐ SIBLING ☐ OTHER:...............

TROOP ROLE(S): ☐ TREASURER ☐ COOKIE MANAGER ☐ FALL PRODUCT MANAGER ☐ CHAPERONE ☐ DRIVER ☐ GENERAL HELPER ☐ OTHER:...............

PHONE: (......)........... EMAIL:................. SPECIAL SKILLS:...............

NOTES:

"A SUCCESSFUL COMPETITION FOR ME IS ALWAYS GOING OUT THERE AND PUTTING 100 PERCENT INTO WHATEVER I'M DOING. IT'S NOT ALWAYS WINNING."

OLYMPIC GYMNAST & MENTAL HEALTH ADVOCATE SIMONE BILES

NAME: ☐ BACKGROUND CHECK

VOLUNTEER TROOP MEMBER: ....'S ☐ PARENT/GUARDIAN ☐ GRANDPARENT ☐ SIBLING ☐ OTHER: ....

TROOP ROLE(S): ☐ TREASURER ☐ COOKIE MANAGER ☐ FALL PRODUCT MANAGER ☐ CHAPERONE ☐ DRIVER ☐ GENERAL HELPER ☐ OTHER: ....

PHONE: (......) .... EMAIL: .... SPECIAL SKILLS: ....

NOTES:

NAME: ☐ BACKGROUND CHECK

VOLUNTEER TROOP MEMBER: ....'S ☐ PARENT/GUARDIAN ☐ GRANDPARENT ☐ SIBLING ☐ OTHER: ....

TROOP ROLE(S): ☐ TREASURER ☐ COOKIE MANAGER ☐ FALL PRODUCT MANAGER ☐ CHAPERONE ☐ DRIVER ☐ GENERAL HELPER ☐ OTHER: ....

PHONE: (......) .... EMAIL: .... SPECIAL SKILLS: ....

NOTES:

NAME: ☐ BACKGROUND CHECK

VOLUNTEER TROOP MEMBER: ....'S ☐ PARENT/GUARDIAN ☐ GRANDPARENT ☐ SIBLING ☐ OTHER: ....

TROOP ROLE(S): ☐ TREASURER ☐ COOKIE MANAGER ☐ FALL PRODUCT MANAGER ☐ CHAPERONE ☐ DRIVER ☐ GENERAL HELPER ☐ OTHER: ....

PHONE: (......) .... EMAIL: .... SPECIAL SKILLS: ....

NOTES:

NAME: ☐ BACKGROUND CHECK

VOLUNTEER TROOP MEMBER: ....'S ☐ PARENT/GUARDIAN ☐ GRANDPARENT ☐ SIBLING ☐ OTHER: ....

TROOP ROLE(S): ☐ TREASURER ☐ COOKIE MANAGER ☐ FALL PRODUCT MANAGER ☐ CHAPERONE ☐ DRIVER ☐ GENERAL HELPER ☐ OTHER: ....

PHONE: (......) .... EMAIL: .... SPECIAL SKILLS: ....

NOTES:

NAME: ☐ BACKGROUND CHECK

VOLUNTEER TROOP MEMBER: ....'S ☐ PARENT/GUARDIAN ☐ GRANDPARENT ☐ SIBLING ☐ OTHER: ....

TROOP ROLE(S): ☐ TREASURER ☐ COOKIE MANAGER ☐ FALL PRODUCT MANAGER ☐ CHAPERONE ☐ DRIVER ☐ GENERAL HELPER ☐ OTHER: ....

PHONE: (......) .... EMAIL: .... SPECIAL SKILLS: ....

NOTES:

VOLUNTEER CONTACT INFORMATION (CONTINUED)

NAME: .... ☐ BACKGROUND CHECK

VOLUNTEER TROOP MEMBER:..'S ☐ PARENT/GUARDIAN ☐ GRANDPARENT ☐ SIBLING ☐ OTHER:..................

TROOP ROLE(S): ☐ TREASURER ☐ COOKIE MANAGER ☐ FALL PRODUCT MANAGER ☐ CHAPERONE ☐ DRIVER ☐ GENERAL HELPER ☐ OTHER:..................

PHONE: (.......)................ EMAIL:.............................. SPECIAL SKILLS:..................

NOTES:

NAME: .... ☐ BACKGROUND CHECK

VOLUNTEER TROOP MEMBER:..'S ☐ PARENT/GUARDIAN ☐ GRANDPARENT ☐ SIBLING ☐ OTHER:..................

TROOP ROLE(S): ☐ TREASURER ☐ COOKIE MANAGER ☐ FALL PRODUCT MANAGER ☐ CHAPERONE ☐ DRIVER ☐ GENERAL HELPER ☐ OTHER:..................

PHONE: (.......)................ EMAIL:.............................. SPECIAL SKILLS:..................

NOTES:

NAME: .... ☐ BACKGROUND CHECK

VOLUNTEER TROOP MEMBER:..'S ☐ PARENT/GUARDIAN ☐ GRANDPARENT ☐ SIBLING ☐ OTHER:..................

TROOP ROLE(S): ☐ TREASURER ☐ COOKIE MANAGER ☐ FALL PRODUCT MANAGER ☐ CHAPERONE ☐ DRIVER ☐ GENERAL HELPER ☐ OTHER:..................

PHONE: (.......)................ EMAIL:.............................. SPECIAL SKILLS:..................

NOTES:

NAME: .... ☐ BACKGROUND CHECK

VOLUNTEER TROOP MEMBER:..'S ☐ PARENT/GUARDIAN ☐ GRANDPARENT ☐ SIBLING ☐ OTHER:..................

TROOP ROLE(S): ☐ TREASURER ☐ COOKIE MANAGER ☐ FALL PRODUCT MANAGER ☐ CHAPERONE ☐ DRIVER ☐ GENERAL HELPER ☐ OTHER:..................

PHONE: (.......)................ EMAIL:.............................. SPECIAL SKILLS:..................

NOTES:

NAME: .... ☐ BACKGROUND CHECK

VOLUNTEER TROOP MEMBER:..'S ☐ PARENT/GUARDIAN ☐ GRANDPARENT ☐ SIBLING ☐ OTHER:..................

TROOP ROLE(S): ☐ TREASURER ☐ COOKIE MANAGER ☐ FALL PRODUCT MANAGER ☐ CHAPERONE ☐ DRIVER ☐ GENERAL HELPER ☐ OTHER:..................

PHONE: (.......)................ EMAIL:.............................. SPECIAL SKILLS:..................

NOTES:

NAME: ☐ BACKGROUND CHECK

VOLUNTEER TROOP MEMBER:...'S ☐ PARENT/GUARDIAN ☐ GRANDPARENT ☐ SIBLING ☐ OTHER:.......

TROOP ROLE(S): ☐ TREASURER ☐ COOKIE MANAGER ☐ FALL PRODUCT MANAGER ☐ CHAPERONE ☐ DRIVER ☐ GENERAL HELPER ☐ OTHER:.......

PHONE: (.......)................ EMAIL:.. SPECIAL SKILLS:.......

NOTES:

NAME: ☐ BACKGROUND CHECK

VOLUNTEER TROOP MEMBER:...'S ☐ PARENT/GUARDIAN ☐ GRANDPARENT ☐ SIBLING ☐ OTHER:.......

TROOP ROLE(S): ☐ TREASURER ☐ COOKIE MANAGER ☐ FALL PRODUCT MANAGER ☐ CHAPERONE ☐ DRIVER ☐ GENERAL HELPER ☐ OTHER:.......

PHONE: (.......)................ EMAIL:.. SPECIAL SKILLS:.......

NOTES:

NAME: ☐ BACKGROUND CHECK

VOLUNTEER TROOP MEMBER:...'S ☐ PARENT/GUARDIAN ☐ GRANDPARENT ☐ SIBLING ☐ OTHER:.......

TROOP ROLE(S): ☐ TREASURER ☐ COOKIE MANAGER ☐ FALL PRODUCT MANAGER ☐ CHAPERONE ☐ DRIVER ☐ GENERAL HELPER ☐ OTHER:.......

PHONE: (.......)................ EMAIL:.. SPECIAL SKILLS:.......

NOTES:

NAME: ☐ BACKGROUND CHECK

VOLUNTEER TROOP MEMBER:...'S ☐ PARENT/GUARDIAN ☐ GRANDPARENT ☐ SIBLING ☐ OTHER:.......

TROOP ROLE(S): ☐ TREASURER ☐ COOKIE MANAGER ☐ FALL PRODUCT MANAGER ☐ CHAPERONE ☐ DRIVER ☐ GENERAL HELPER ☐ OTHER:.......

PHONE: (.......)................ EMAIL:.. SPECIAL SKILLS:.......

NOTES:

NAME: ☐ BACKGROUND CHECK

VOLUNTEER TROOP MEMBER:...'S ☐ PARENT/GUARDIAN ☐ GRANDPARENT ☐ SIBLING ☐ OTHER:.......

TROOP ROLE(S): ☐ TREASURER ☐ COOKIE MANAGER ☐ FALL PRODUCT MANAGER ☐ CHAPERONE ☐ DRIVER ☐ GENERAL HELPER ☐ OTHER:.......

PHONE: (.......)................ EMAIL:.. SPECIAL SKILLS:.......

NOTES:

VOLUNTEER CONTACT INFORMATION (CONTINUED)

NAME: ☐ BACKGROUND CHECK

VOLUNTEER TROOP MEMBER:..'S ☐PARENT/GUARDIAN ☐GRANDPARENT ☐SIBLING ☐OTHER:...............

TROOP ROLE(S): ☐TREASURER ☐COOKIE MANAGER ☐FALL PRODUCT MANAGER ☐CHAPERONE ☐DRIVER ☐GENERAL HELPER ☐OTHER:...............

PHONE: (......)............... EMAIL:............................... SPECIAL SKILLS:...............

NOTES:

NAME: ☐ BACKGROUND CHECK

VOLUNTEER TROOP MEMBER:..'S ☐PARENT/GUARDIAN ☐GRANDPARENT ☐SIBLING ☐OTHER:...............

TROOP ROLE(S): ☐TREASURER ☐COOKIE MANAGER ☐FALL PRODUCT MANAGER ☐CHAPERONE ☐DRIVER ☐GENERAL HELPER ☐OTHER:...............

PHONE: (......)............... EMAIL:............................... SPECIAL SKILLS:...............

NOTES:

NAME: ☐ BACKGROUND CHECK

VOLUNTEER TROOP MEMBER:..'S ☐PARENT/GUARDIAN ☐GRANDPARENT ☐SIBLING ☐OTHER:...............

TROOP ROLE(S): ☐TREASURER ☐COOKIE MANAGER ☐FALL PRODUCT MANAGER ☐CHAPERONE ☐DRIVER ☐GENERAL HELPER ☐OTHER:...............

PHONE: (......)............... EMAIL:............................... SPECIAL SKILLS:...............

NOTES:

NAME: ☐ BACKGROUND CHECK

VOLUNTEER TROOP MEMBER:..'S ☐PARENT/GUARDIAN ☐GRANDPARENT ☐SIBLING ☐OTHER:...............

TROOP ROLE(S): ☐TREASURER ☐COOKIE MANAGER ☐FALL PRODUCT MANAGER ☐CHAPERONE ☐DRIVER ☐GENERAL HELPER ☐OTHER:...............

PHONE: (......)............... EMAIL:............................... SPECIAL SKILLS:...............

NOTES:

NAME: ☐ BACKGROUND CHECK

VOLUNTEER TROOP MEMBER:..'S ☐PARENT/GUARDIAN ☐GRANDPARENT ☐SIBLING ☐OTHER:...............

TROOP ROLE(S): ☐TREASURER ☐COOKIE MANAGER ☐FALL PRODUCT MANAGER ☐CHAPERONE ☐DRIVER ☐GENERAL HELPER ☐OTHER:...............

PHONE: (......)............... EMAIL:............................... SPECIAL SKILLS:...............

NOTES:

SERVICE UNIT:

POSITION:

NAME: ....

PHONE: (......) ....

EMAIL: ....

NOTES:

POSITION:

NAME: ....

PHONE: (......) ....

EMAIL: ....

NOTES:

POSITION:

NAME: ....

PHONE: (......) ....

EMAIL: ....

NOTES:

POSITION:

NAME: ....

PHONE: (......) ....

EMAIL: ....

NOTES:

POSITION:

NAME: ....

PHONE: (......) ....

EMAIL: ....

NOTES:

POSITION:

NAME: ....

PHONE: (......) ....

EMAIL: ....

NOTES:

POSITION:

NAME: ....

PHONE: (......) ....

EMAIL: ....

NOTES:

POSITION:

NAME: ....

PHONE: (......) ....

EMAIL: ....

NOTES:

COUNCIL:

PHONE: (......).......................... FAX: (......)......................... EMAIL(S):...

SERVICE CENTER ADDRESS:... SERVICE CENTER HOURS:...

SHOP ADDRESS:.. SHOP HOURS:..

WEBSITE:................................... SOCIAL MEDIA:...

NOTES:

POSITION:

NAME:...

PHONE: (......)..

EMAIL:..

NOTES:

POSITION:

NAME:...

PHONE: (......)..

EMAIL:..

NOTES:

POSITION:

NAME:...

PHONE: (......)..

EMAIL:..

NOTES:

POSITION:

NAME:...

PHONE: (......)..

EMAIL:..

NOTES:

POSITION:

NAME:...

PHONE: (......)..

EMAIL:..

NOTES:

POSITION:

NAME:...

PHONE: (......)..

EMAIL:..

NOTES:

TROOP ROSTER

NAME: .... BIRTHDAY: ...... / ...... / ...... AGE: ....

PHONE: (......) .... EMAIL: .... SCHOOL: .... GRADE: ....

ADDRESS: .... LIVES WITH: ....

SHIRT SIZE: .... ALLERGIES: .... ON FILE: ☐ REGISTRATION ☐ HEALTH HISTORY ☐ PERMISSION SLIP ☐ OTHER: ....

PARENT/GUARDIAN: .... PHONE: (......) .... EMAIL: ....

PARENT/GUARDIAN: .... PHONE: (......) .... EMAIL: ....

NOTES:

☐ DAISY ☐ BROWNIE ☐ JUNIOR ☐ CADETTE ☐ SENIOR ☐ AMBASSADOR

NAME: .... BIRTHDAY: ...... / ...... / ...... AGE: ....

PHONE: (......) .... EMAIL: .... SCHOOL: .... GRADE: ....

ADDRESS: .... LIVES WITH: ....

SHIRT SIZE: .... ALLERGIES: .... ON FILE: ☐ REGISTRATION ☐ HEALTH HISTORY ☐ PERMISSION SLIP ☐ OTHER: ....

PARENT/GUARDIAN: .... PHONE: (......) .... EMAIL: ....

PARENT/GUARDIAN: .... PHONE: (......) .... EMAIL: ....

NOTES:

☐ DAISY ☐ BROWNIE ☐ JUNIOR ☐ CADETTE ☐ SENIOR ☐ AMBASSADOR

NAME: .... BIRTHDAY: ...... / ...... / ...... AGE: ....

PHONE: (......) .... EMAIL: .... SCHOOL: .... GRADE: ....

ADDRESS: .... LIVES WITH: ....

SHIRT SIZE: .... ALLERGIES: .... ON FILE: ☐ REGISTRATION ☐ HEALTH HISTORY ☐ PERMISSION SLIP ☐ OTHER: ....

PARENT/GUARDIAN: .... PHONE: (......) .... EMAIL: ....

PARENT/GUARDIAN: .... PHONE: (......) .... EMAIL: ....

NOTES:

☐ DAISY ☐ BROWNIE ☐ JUNIOR ☐ CADETTE ☐ SENIOR ☐ AMBASSADOR

TROOP ROSTER (CONTINUED)

NAME: .... BIRTHDAY: ...... / ...... / ...... AGE: ....

PHONE: (......) .... EMAIL: .... SCHOOL: .... GRADE: ....

ADDRESS: .... LIVES WITH: ....

SHIRT SIZE: .... ALLERGIES: .... ON FILE: ☐ REGISTRATION ☐ HEALTH HISTORY ☐ PERMISSION SLIP ☐ OTHER: ....

PARENT/GUARDIAN: .... PHONE: (......) .... EMAIL: ....

PARENT/GUARDIAN: .... PHONE: (......) .... EMAIL: ....

NOTES: ....

☐ DAISY ☐ BROWNIE ☐ JUNIOR ☐ CADETTE ☐ SENIOR ☐ AMBASSADOR

NAME: .... BIRTHDAY: ...... / ...... / ...... AGE: ....

PHONE: (......) .... EMAIL: .... SCHOOL: .... GRADE: ....

ADDRESS: .... LIVES WITH: ....

SHIRT SIZE: .... ALLERGIES: .... ON FILE: ☐ REGISTRATION ☐ HEALTH HISTORY ☐ PERMISSION SLIP ☐ OTHER: ....

PARENT/GUARDIAN: .... PHONE: (......) .... EMAIL: ....

PARENT/GUARDIAN: .... PHONE: (......) .... EMAIL: ....

NOTES: ....

☐ DAISY ☐ BROWNIE ☐ JUNIOR ☐ CADETTE ☐ SENIOR ☐ AMBASSADOR

NAME: .... BIRTHDAY: ...... / ...... / ...... AGE: ....

PHONE: (......) .... EMAIL: .... SCHOOL: .... GRADE: ....

ADDRESS: .... LIVES WITH: ....

SHIRT SIZE: .... ALLERGIES: .... ON FILE: ☐ REGISTRATION ☐ HEALTH HISTORY ☐ PERMISSION SLIP ☐ OTHER: ....

PARENT/GUARDIAN: .... PHONE: (......) .... EMAIL: ....

PARENT/GUARDIAN: .... PHONE: (......) .... EMAIL: ....

NOTES: ....

☐ DAISY ☐ BROWNIE ☐ JUNIOR ☐ CADETTE ☐ SENIOR ☐ AMBASSADOR

NAME: .... BIRTHDAY: ...... / ...... / ...... AGE: ....

PHONE: (......) .... EMAIL: .... SCHOOL: .... GRADE: ....

ADDRESS: .... LIVES WITH: ....

SHIRT SIZE: .... ALLERGIES: .... ON FILE: ☐ REGISTRATION ☐ HEALTH HISTORY ☐ PERMISSION SLIP ☐ OTHER: ....

PARENT/GUARDIAN: .... PHONE: (......) .... EMAIL: ....

PARENT/GUARDIAN: .... PHONE: (......) .... EMAIL: ....

NOTES:

☐ DAISY ☐ BROWNIE ☐ JUNIOR ☐ CADETTE ☐ SENIOR ☐ AMBASSADOR

NAME: .... BIRTHDAY: ...... / ...... / ...... AGE: ....

PHONE: (......) .... EMAIL: .... SCHOOL: .... GRADE: ....

ADDRESS: .... LIVES WITH: ....

SHIRT SIZE: .... ALLERGIES: .... ON FILE: ☐ REGISTRATION ☐ HEALTH HISTORY ☐ PERMISSION SLIP ☐ OTHER: ....

PARENT/GUARDIAN: .... PHONE: (......) .... EMAIL: ....

PARENT/GUARDIAN: .... PHONE: (......) .... EMAIL: ....

NOTES:

☐ DAISY ☐ BROWNIE ☐ JUNIOR ☐ CADETTE ☐ SENIOR ☐ AMBASSADOR

NAME: .... BIRTHDAY: ...... / ...... / ...... AGE: ....

PHONE: (......) .... EMAIL: .... SCHOOL: .... GRADE: ....

ADDRESS: .... LIVES WITH: ....

SHIRT SIZE: .... ALLERGIES: .... ON FILE: ☐ REGISTRATION ☐ HEALTH HISTORY ☐ PERMISSION SLIP ☐ OTHER: ....

PARENT/GUARDIAN: .... PHONE: (......) .... EMAIL: ....

PARENT/GUARDIAN: .... PHONE: (......) .... EMAIL: ....

NOTES:

☐ DAISY ☐ BROWNIE ☐ JUNIOR ☐ CADETTE ☐ SENIOR ☐ AMBASSADOR

TROOP ROSTER (CONTINUED)

NAME: .... BIRTHDAY: ...... / ...... / ...... AGE: ....

PHONE: (......) .... EMAIL: .... SCHOOL: .... GRADE: ....

ADDRESS: .... LIVES WITH: ....

SHIRT SIZE: .... ALLERGIES: .... ON FILE: ☐ REGISTRATION ☐ HEALTH HISTORY ☐ PERMISSION SLIP ☐ OTHER: ....

PARENT/GUARDIAN: .... PHONE: (......) .... EMAIL: ....

PARENT/GUARDIAN: .... PHONE: (......) .... EMAIL: ....

NOTES: ....

☐ DAISY ☐ BROWNIE ☐ JUNIOR ☐ CADETTE ☐ SENIOR ☐ AMBASSADOR

NAME: .... BIRTHDAY: ...... / ...... / ...... AGE: ....

PHONE: (......) .... EMAIL: .... SCHOOL: .... GRADE: ....

ADDRESS: .... LIVES WITH: ....

SHIRT SIZE: .... ALLERGIES: .... ON FILE: ☐ REGISTRATION ☐ HEALTH HISTORY ☐ PERMISSION SLIP ☐ OTHER: ....

PARENT/GUARDIAN: .... PHONE: (......) .... EMAIL: ....

PARENT/GUARDIAN: .... PHONE: (......) .... EMAIL: ....

NOTES: ....

☐ DAISY ☐ BROWNIE ☐ JUNIOR ☐ CADETTE ☐ SENIOR ☐ AMBASSADOR

NAME: .... BIRTHDAY: ...... / ...... / ...... AGE: ....

PHONE: (......) .... EMAIL: .... SCHOOL: .... GRADE: ....

ADDRESS: .... LIVES WITH: ....

SHIRT SIZE: .... ALLERGIES: .... ON FILE: ☐ REGISTRATION ☐ HEALTH HISTORY ☐ PERMISSION SLIP ☐ OTHER: ....

PARENT/GUARDIAN: .... PHONE: (......) .... EMAIL: ....

PARENT/GUARDIAN: .... PHONE: (......) .... EMAIL: ....

NOTES: ....

☐ DAISY ☐ BROWNIE ☐ JUNIOR ☐ CADETTE ☐ SENIOR ☐ AMBASSADOR

"WE CLOSE THE DIVIDE BECAUSE WE KNOW TO PUT OUR FUTURE FIRST / WE MUST FIRST PUT OUR DIFFERENCES ASIDE."

AWARD-WINNING POET AMANDA GORMAN

NAME: BIRTHDAY: ___/___/___ AGE: _____

PHONE: (___) _____ EMAIL: _____ SCHOOL: _____ GRADE: _____

ADDRESS: _____ LIVES WITH: _____

SHIRT SIZE: _____ ALLERGIES: _____ ON FILE: □ REGISTRATION □ HEALTH HISTORY □ PERMISSION SLIP □ OTHER: _____

PARENT/GUARDIAN: _____ PHONE: (___) _____ EMAIL: _____

PARENT/GUARDIAN: _____ PHONE: (___) _____ EMAIL: _____

NOTES:

□ DAISY □ BROWNIE □ JUNIOR □ CADETTE □ SENIOR □ AMBASSADOR

NAME: BIRTHDAY: ___/___/___ AGE: _____

PHONE: (___) _____ EMAIL: _____ SCHOOL: _____ GRADE: _____

ADDRESS: _____ LIVES WITH: _____

SHIRT SIZE: _____ ALLERGIES: _____ ON FILE: □ REGISTRATION □ HEALTH HISTORY □ PERMISSION SLIP □ OTHER: _____

PARENT/GUARDIAN: _____ PHONE: (___) _____ EMAIL: _____

PARENT/GUARDIAN: _____ PHONE: (___) _____ EMAIL: _____

NOTES:

□ DAISY □ BROWNIE □ JUNIOR □ CADETTE □ SENIOR □ AMBASSADOR

NAME: BIRTHDAY: ___/___/___ AGE: _____

PHONE: (___) _____ EMAIL: _____ SCHOOL: _____ GRADE: _____

ADDRESS: _____ LIVES WITH: _____

SHIRT SIZE: _____ ALLERGIES: _____ ON FILE: □ REGISTRATION □ HEALTH HISTORY □ PERMISSION SLIP □ OTHER: _____

PARENT/GUARDIAN: _____ PHONE: (___) _____ EMAIL: _____

PARENT/GUARDIAN: _____ PHONE: (___) _____ EMAIL: _____

NOTES:

□ DAISY □ BROWNIE □ JUNIOR □ CADETTE □ SENIOR □ AMBASSADOR

TROOP ROSTER (CONTINUED)

NAME: .... BIRTHDAY: ...... / ...... / ...... AGE: ....

PHONE: (......) .... EMAIL: .... SCHOOL: .... GRADE: ....

ADDRESS: .... LIVES WITH: ....

SHIRT SIZE: .... ALLERGIES: .... ON FILE: ☐ REGISTRATION ☐ HEALTH HISTORY ☐ PERMISSION SLIP ☐ OTHER: ....

PARENT/GUARDIAN: .... PHONE: (......) .... EMAIL: ....

PARENT/GUARDIAN: .... PHONE: (......) .... EMAIL: ....

NOTES:

☐ DAISY ☐ BROWNIE ☐ JUNIOR ☐ CADETTE ☐ SENIOR ☐ AMBASSADOR

NAME: .... BIRTHDAY: ...... / ...... / ...... AGE: ....

PHONE: (......) .... EMAIL: .... SCHOOL: .... GRADE: ....

ADDRESS: .... LIVES WITH: ....

SHIRT SIZE: .... ALLERGIES: .... ON FILE: ☐ REGISTRATION ☐ HEALTH HISTORY ☐ PERMISSION SLIP ☐ OTHER: ....

PARENT/GUARDIAN: .... PHONE: (......) .... EMAIL: ....

PARENT/GUARDIAN: .... PHONE: (......) .... EMAIL: ....

NOTES:

☐ DAISY ☐ BROWNIE ☐ JUNIOR ☐ CADETTE ☐ SENIOR ☐ AMBASSADOR

NAME: .... BIRTHDAY: ...... / ...... / ...... AGE: ....

PHONE: (......) .... EMAIL: .... SCHOOL: .... GRADE: ....

ADDRESS: .... LIVES WITH: ....

SHIRT SIZE: .... ALLERGIES: .... ON FILE: ☐ REGISTRATION ☐ HEALTH HISTORY ☐ PERMISSION SLIP ☐ OTHER: ....

PARENT/GUARDIAN: .... PHONE: (......) .... EMAIL: ....

PARENT/GUARDIAN: .... PHONE: (......) .... EMAIL: ....

NOTES:

☐ DAISY ☐ BROWNIE ☐ JUNIOR ☐ CADETTE ☐ SENIOR ☐ AMBASSADOR

"IT'S IMPORTANT TO ME TO CONSTANTLY CHALLENGE MYSELF, TO UNDERSTAND DIFFERENT VIEWPOINTS, ... SO I CAN FEEL QUALIFIED IN WHAT I SAY."

ACTRESS & ANTI-RACISM ADVOCATE YARA SHAHIDI

NAME: .... BIRTHDAY: ...... / ...... / ...... AGE: ....

PHONE: (......) .... EMAIL: .... SCHOOL: .... GRADE: ....

ADDRESS: .... LIVES WITH: ....

SHIRT SIZE: .... ALLERGIES: .... ON FILE: ☐ REGISTRATION ☐ HEALTH HISTORY ☐ PERMISSION SLIP ☐ OTHER: ....

PARENT/GUARDIAN: .... PHONE: (......) .... EMAIL: ....

PARENT/GUARDIAN: .... PHONE: (......) .... EMAIL: ....

NOTES: ....

☐ DAISY ☐ BROWNIE ☐ JUNIOR ☐ CADETTE ☐ SENIOR ☐ AMBASSADOR

NAME: .... BIRTHDAY: ...... / ...... / ...... AGE: ....

PHONE: (......) .... EMAIL: .... SCHOOL: .... GRADE: ....

ADDRESS: .... LIVES WITH: ....

SHIRT SIZE: .... ALLERGIES: .... ON FILE: ☐ REGISTRATION ☐ HEALTH HISTORY ☐ PERMISSION SLIP ☐ OTHER: ....

PARENT/GUARDIAN: .... PHONE: (......) .... EMAIL: ....

PARENT/GUARDIAN: .... PHONE: (......) .... EMAIL: ....

NOTES: ....

☐ DAISY ☐ BROWNIE ☐ JUNIOR ☐ CADETTE ☐ SENIOR ☐ AMBASSADOR

NAME: .... BIRTHDAY: ...... / ...... / ...... AGE: ....

PHONE: (......) .... EMAIL: .... SCHOOL: .... GRADE: ....

ADDRESS: .... LIVES WITH: ....

SHIRT SIZE: .... ALLERGIES: .... ON FILE: ☐ REGISTRATION ☐ HEALTH HISTORY ☐ PERMISSION SLIP ☐ OTHER: ....

PARENT/GUARDIAN: .... PHONE: (......) .... EMAIL: ....

PARENT/GUARDIAN: .... PHONE: (......) .... EMAIL: ....

NOTES: ....

☐ DAISY ☐ BROWNIE ☐ JUNIOR ☐ CADETTE ☐ SENIOR ☐ AMBASSADOR

TROOP ROSTER (CONTINUED)

NAME: .... BIRTHDAY: ...... / ...... / ...... AGE: ....

PHONE: (......) .... EMAIL: .... SCHOOL: .... GRADE: ....

ADDRESS: .... LIVES WITH: ....

SHIRT SIZE: .... ALLERGIES: .... ON FILE: ☐ REGISTRATION ☐ HEALTH HISTORY ☐ PERMISSION SLIP ☐ OTHER: ....

PARENT/GUARDIAN: .... PHONE: (......) .... EMAIL: ....

PARENT/GUARDIAN: .... PHONE: (......) .... EMAIL: ....

NOTES: ....

☐ DAISY ☐ BROWNIE ☐ JUNIOR ☐ CADETTE ☐ SENIOR ☐ AMBASSADOR

NAME: .... BIRTHDAY: ...... / ...... / ...... AGE: ....

PHONE: (......) .... EMAIL: .... SCHOOL: .... GRADE: ....

ADDRESS: .... LIVES WITH: ....

SHIRT SIZE: .... ALLERGIES: .... ON FILE: ☐ REGISTRATION ☐ HEALTH HISTORY ☐ PERMISSION SLIP ☐ OTHER: ....

PARENT/GUARDIAN: .... PHONE: (......) .... EMAIL: ....

PARENT/GUARDIAN: .... PHONE: (......) .... EMAIL: ....

NOTES: ....

☐ DAISY ☐ BROWNIE ☐ JUNIOR ☐ CADETTE ☐ SENIOR ☐ AMBASSADOR

NAME: .... BIRTHDAY: ...... / ...... / ...... AGE: ....

PHONE: (......) .... EMAIL: .... SCHOOL: .... GRADE: ....

ADDRESS: .... LIVES WITH: ....

SHIRT SIZE: .... ALLERGIES: .... ON FILE: ☐ REGISTRATION ☐ HEALTH HISTORY ☐ PERMISSION SLIP ☐ OTHER: ....

PARENT/GUARDIAN: .... PHONE: (......) .... EMAIL: ....

PARENT/GUARDIAN: .... PHONE: (......) .... EMAIL: ....

NOTES: ....

☐ DAISY ☐ BROWNIE ☐ JUNIOR ☐ CADETTE ☐ SENIOR ☐ AMBASSADOR

NAME: .... BIRTHDAY: ..... / ..... / ..... AGE: ....

PHONE: (......) .... EMAIL: .... SCHOOL: .... GRADE: ....

ADDRESS: .... LIVES WITH: ....

SHIRT SIZE: .... ALLERGIES: .... ON FILE: ☐ REGISTRATION ☐ HEALTH HISTORY ☐ PERMISSION SLIP ☐ OTHER: ....

PARENT/GUARDIAN: .... PHONE: (......) .... EMAIL: ....

PARENT/GUARDIAN: .... PHONE: (......) .... EMAIL: ....

NOTES:

☐ DAISY ☐ BROWNIE ☐ JUNIOR ☐ CADETTE ☐ SENIOR ☐ AMBASSADOR

NAME: .... BIRTHDAY: ..... / ..... / ..... AGE: ....

PHONE: (......) .... EMAIL: .... SCHOOL: .... GRADE: ....

ADDRESS: .... LIVES WITH: ....

SHIRT SIZE: .... ALLERGIES: .... ON FILE: ☐ REGISTRATION ☐ HEALTH HISTORY ☐ PERMISSION SLIP ☐ OTHER: ....

PARENT/GUARDIAN: .... PHONE: (......) .... EMAIL: ....

PARENT/GUARDIAN: .... PHONE: (......) .... EMAIL: ....

NOTES:

☐ DAISY ☐ BROWNIE ☐ JUNIOR ☐ CADETTE ☐ SENIOR ☐ AMBASSADOR

NAME: .... BIRTHDAY: ..... / ..... / ..... AGE: ....

PHONE: (......) .... EMAIL: .... SCHOOL: .... GRADE: ....

ADDRESS: .... LIVES WITH: ....

SHIRT SIZE: .... ALLERGIES: .... ON FILE: ☐ REGISTRATION ☐ HEALTH HISTORY ☐ PERMISSION SLIP ☐ OTHER: ....

PARENT/GUARDIAN: .... PHONE: (......) .... EMAIL: ....

PARENT/GUARDIAN: .... PHONE: (......) .... EMAIL: ....

NOTES:

☐ DAISY ☐ BROWNIE ☐ JUNIOR ☐ CADETTE ☐ SENIOR ☐ AMBASSADOR

TROOP ROSTER (CONTINUED)

NAME: .... BIRTHDAY: ...... / ...... / ...... AGE: ....

PHONE: (......) .... EMAIL: .... SCHOOL: .... GRADE: ....

ADDRESS: .... LIVES WITH: ....

SHIRT SIZE: .... ALLERGIES: .... ON FILE: ☐ REGISTRATION ☐ HEALTH HISTORY ☐ PERMISSION SLIP ☐ OTHER: ....

PARENT/GUARDIAN: .... PHONE: (......) .... EMAIL: ....

PARENT/GUARDIAN: .... PHONE: (......) .... EMAIL: ....

NOTES: ....

☐ DAISY ☐ BROWNIE ☐ JUNIOR ☐ CADETTE ☐ SENIOR ☐ AMBASSADOR

NAME: .... BIRTHDAY: ...... / ...... / ...... AGE: ....

PHONE: (......) .... EMAIL: .... SCHOOL: .... GRADE: ....

ADDRESS: .... LIVES WITH: ....

SHIRT SIZE: .... ALLERGIES: .... ON FILE: ☐ REGISTRATION ☐ HEALTH HISTORY ☐ PERMISSION SLIP ☐ OTHER: ....

PARENT/GUARDIAN: .... PHONE: (......) .... EMAIL: ....

PARENT/GUARDIAN: .... PHONE: (......) .... EMAIL: ....

NOTES: ....

☐ DAISY ☐ BROWNIE ☐ JUNIOR ☐ CADETTE ☐ SENIOR ☐ AMBASSADOR

NAME: .... BIRTHDAY: ...... / ...... / ...... AGE: ....

PHONE: (......) .... EMAIL: .... SCHOOL: .... GRADE: ....

ADDRESS: .... LIVES WITH: ....

SHIRT SIZE: .... ALLERGIES: .... ON FILE: ☐ REGISTRATION ☐ HEALTH HISTORY ☐ PERMISSION SLIP ☐ OTHER: ....

PARENT/GUARDIAN: .... PHONE: (......) .... EMAIL: ....

PARENT/GUARDIAN: .... PHONE: (......) .... EMAIL: ....

NOTES: ....

☐ DAISY ☐ BROWNIE ☐ JUNIOR ☐ CADETTE ☐ SENIOR ☐ AMBASSADOR

TROOP BIRTHDAYS

JANUARY	FEBRUARY	MARCH
APRIL	MAY	JUNE
JULY	AUGUST	SEPTEMBER
OCTOBER	NOVEMBER	DECEMBER

SUNDAY	MONDAY	TUESDAY	WEDNESDAY	THURSDAY	FRIDAY	SATURDAY

NOTES:

SUNDAY	MONDAY	TUESDAY	WEDNESDAY	THURSDAY	FRIDAY	SATURDAY

TES:

SUNDAY	MONDAY	TUESDAY	WEDNESDAY	THURSDAY	FRIDAY	SATURDAY

NOTES:

SUNDAY	MONDAY	TUESDAY	WEDNESDAY	THURSDAY	FRIDAY	SATURDAY

ES:

SUNDAY	MONDAY	TUESDAY	WEDNESDAY	THURSDAY	FRIDAY	SATURDAY

NOTES:

SUNDAY	MONDAY	TUESDAY	WEDNESDAY	THURSDAY	FRIDAY	SATURDAY

S:

SUNDAY	MONDAY	TUESDAY	WEDNESDAY	THURSDAY	FRIDAY	SATURDAY

NOTES:

SUNDAY	MONDAY	TUESDAY	WEDNESDAY	THURSDAY	FRIDAY	SATURDAY

ES:

SUNDAY	MONDAY	TUESDAY	WEDNESDAY	THURSDAY	FRIDAY	SATURDAY

NOTES:

SUNDAY	MONDAY	TUESDAY	WEDNESDAY	THURSDAY	FRIDAY	SATURDAY

ES:

SUNDAY	MONDAY	TUESDAY	WEDNESDAY	THURSDAY	FRIDAY	SATURDAY

NOTES:

SUNDAY	MONDAY	TUESDAY	WEDNESDAY	THURSDAY	FRIDAY	SATURDAY

ES:

SUNDAY	MONDAY	TUESDAY	WEDNESDAY	THURSDAY	FRIDAY	SATURDAY

NOTES:

SUNDAY	MONDAY	TUESDAY	WEDNESDAY	THURSDAY	FRIDAY	SATURDAY

s:

MEETING PLANNER

DATE:

MEETING DETAILS

TIME: .... LOCATION: .... BADGE/JOURNEY/AWARD: ....

MEETING GOAL/THEME: ....

PRE-MEETING PREP:

SUPPLIES:
- ☐
- ☐
- ☐
- ☐
- ☐

VOLUNTEERS:
- ☐
- ☐
- ☐
- ☐
- ☐

REMINDERS:

MEETING STRUCTURE:

START-UP ACTIVITY:

_____

OPENING:

_____

BUSINESS:

_____

ACTIVITIES:

(1)

(2)

(3)

(4)

(5)

_____

CLEAN-UP & CLOSING:

NEXT MEETING:

REFLECTION:

DURING THIS MEETING, THE GIRLS...
☐ DISCOVERED ☐ CONNECTED ☐ TOOK ACTION

OUR ACTIVITIES WERE...
☐ GIRL-LED ☐ HANDS-ON ☐ COOPERATIVE

ATTENDANCE:
LOW ○ ○ ○ ○ ○ HIGH

ENJOYMENT:
LOW ○ ○ ○ ○ ○ HIGH

ENGAGEMENT:
LOW ○ ○ ○ ○ ○ HIGH

WHAT WAS MOST SUCCESSFUL?

WHAT COULD IMPROVE?

MEETING PLANNER

DATE:

MEETING DETAILS

TIME: ....   LOCATION: ....   BADGE/JOURNEY/AWARD: ....

MEETING GOAL/THEME: ....

PRE-MEETING PREP:

SUPPLIES:
- ☐
- ☐
- ☐
- ☐
- ☐

VOLUNTEERS:
- ☐
- ☐
- ☐
- ☐
- ☐

REMINDERS:

MEETING STRUCTURE:

START-UP ACTIVITY:

_____

OPENING:

_____

BUSINESS:

_____

ACTIVITIES:

(1)

(2)

(3)

(4)

(5)

_____

CLEAN-UP & CLOSING:

NEXT MEETING:

REFLECTION:

DURING THIS MEETING, THE GIRLS...
☐ DISCOVERED ☐ CONNECTED ☐ TOOK ACTION

OUR ACTIVITIES WERE...
☐ GIRL-LED ☐ HANDS-ON ☐ COOPERATIVE

ATTENDANCE:
LOW ○ ○ ○ ○ ○ HIGH

ENJOYMENT:
LOW ○ ○ ○ ○ ○ HIGH

ENGAGEMENT:
LOW ○ ○ ○ ○ ○ HIGH

WHAT WAS MOST SUCCESSFUL?

WHAT COULD IMPROVE?

MEETING PLANNER

DATE:

MEETING DETAILS

TIME: .... LOCATION: .... BADGE/JOURNEY/AWARD: ....

MEETING GOAL/THEME: ....

PRE-MEETING PREP:

SUPPLIES:

- ☐
- ☐
- ☐
- ☐
- ☐

VOLUNTEERS:

- ☐
- ☐
- ☐
- ☐
- ☐

REMINDERS:

MEETING STRUCTURE:

START-UP ACTIVITY:

_____

OPENING:

_____

BUSINESS:

_____

ACTIVITIES:

(1)

(2)

(3)

(4)

(5)

_____

CLEAN-UP & CLOSING:

NEXT MEETING:

REFLECTION:

DURING THIS MEETING, THE GIRLS...
☐ DISCOVERED ☐ CONNECTED ☐ TOOK ACTION

OUR ACTIVITIES WERE...
☐ GIRL-LED ☐ HANDS-ON ☐ COOPERATIVE

ATTENDANCE:
LOW ◯ ◯ ◯ ◯ ◯ HIGH

ENJOYMENT:
LOW ◯ ◯ ◯ ◯ ◯ HIGH

ENGAGEMENT:
LOW ◯ ◯ ◯ ◯ ◯ HIGH

WHAT WAS MOST SUCCESSFUL?

WHAT COULD IMPROVE?

MEETING PLANNER

MEETING DETAILS

TIME: ....   LOCATION: ....   BADGE/JOURNEY/AWARD: ....

MEETING GOAL/THEME: ....

PRE-MEETING PREP:

SUPPLIES:
- ☐
- ☐
- ☐
- ☐
- ☐

VOLUNTEERS:
- ☐
- ☐
- ☐
- ☐
- ☐

REMINDERS:

MEETING STRUCTURE:

START-UP ACTIVITY:

_____

OPENING:

_____

BUSINESS:

_____

ACTIVITIES:

(1)

(2)

(3)

(4)

(5)

_____

CLEAN-UP & CLOSING:

NEXT MEETING:

REFLECTION:

DURING THIS MEETING, THE GIRLS...
☐ DISCOVERED ☐ CONNECTED ☐ TOOK ACTION

OUR ACTIVITIES WERE...
☐ GIRL-LED   ☐ HANDS-ON ☐ COOPERATIVE

ATTENDANCE:
LOW ○ ○ ○ ○ ○ HIGH

ENJOYMENT:
LOW ○ ○ ○ ○ ○ HIGH

ENGAGEMENT:
LOW ○ ○ ○ ○ ○ HIGH

WHAT WAS MOST SUCCESSFUL?

WHAT COULD IMPROVE?

MEETING PLANNER

DATE:

MEETING DETAILS

TIME: .... LOCATION: .... BADGE/JOURNEY/AWARD: ....

MEETING GOAL/THEME: ....

PRE-MEETING PREP:

SUPPLIES:
- ☐
- ☐
- ☐
- ☐
- ☐

VOLUNTEERS:
- ☐
- ☐
- ☐
- ☐
- ☐

REMINDERS:

MEETING STRUCTURE:

START-UP ACTIVITY:

_____

OPENING:

_____

BUSINESS:

_____

ACTIVITIES:

(1)

(2)

(3)

(4)

(5)

_____

CLEAN-UP & CLOSING:

NEXT MEETING:

REFLECTION:

DURING THIS MEETING, THE GIRLS...
☐ DISCOVERED ☐ CONNECTED ☐ TOOK ACTION

OUR ACTIVITIES WERE...
☐ GIRL-LED ☐ HANDS-ON ☐ COOPERATIVE

ATTENDANCE:
LOW ○ ○ ○ ○ ○ HIGH

ENJOYMENT:
LOW ○ ○ ○ ○ ○ HIGH

ENGAGEMENT:
LOW ○ ○ ○ ○ ○ HIGH

WHAT WAS MOST SUCCESSFUL?

WHAT COULD IMPROVE?

MEETING PLANNER

DATE:

MEETING DETAILS

TIME: .... LOCATION: .... BADGE/JOURNEY/AWARD: ....

MEETING GOAL/THEME: ....

PRE-MEETING PREP:

SUPPLIES:
- ☐
- ☐
- ☐
- ☐
- ☐

VOLUNTEERS:
- ☐
- ☐
- ☐
- ☐
- ☐

REMINDERS:

MEETING STRUCTURE:

START-UP ACTIVITY:

_____

OPENING:

_____

BUSINESS:

_____

ACTIVITIES:

(1)

(2)

(3)

(4)

(5)

_____

CLEAN-UP & CLOSING:

NEXT MEETING:

REFLECTION:

DURING THIS MEETING, THE GIRLS...
☐ DISCOVERED ☐ CONNECTED ☐ TOOK ACTION

OUR ACTIVITIES WERE...
☐ GIRL-LED ☐ HANDS-ON ☐ COOPERATIVE

ATTENDANCE:
LOW ○ ○ ○ ○ ○ HIGH

ENJOYMENT:
LOW ○ ○ ○ ○ ○ HIGH

ENGAGEMENT:
LOW ○ ○ ○ ○ ○ HIGH

WHAT WAS MOST SUCCESSFUL?

WHAT COULD IMPROVE?

MEETING PLANNER

DATE:

MEETING DETAILS

TIME: .... LOCATION: .... BADGE/JOURNEY/AWARD: ....

MEETING GOAL/THEME: ....

PRE-MEETING PREP:

SUPPLIES:

- ☐
- ☐
- ☐
- ☐
- ☐

VOLUNTEERS:

- ☐
- ☐
- ☐
- ☐
- ☐

REMINDERS:

MEETING STRUCTURE:

START-UP ACTIVITY:

_____

OPENING:

_____

BUSINESS:

_____

ACTIVITIES:

(1)

(2)

(3)

(4)

(5)

_____

CLEAN-UP & CLOSING:

NEXT MEETING:

REFLECTION:

DURING THIS MEETING, THE GIRLS...
☐ DISCOVERED ☐ CONNECTED ☐ TOOK ACTION

OUR ACTIVITIES WERE...
☐ GIRL-LED ☐ HANDS-ON ☐ COOPERATIVE

ATTENDANCE:
LOW ○ ○ ○ ○ ○ HIGH

ENJOYMENT:
LOW ○ ○ ○ ○ ○ HIGH

ENGAGEMENT:
LOW ○ ○ ○ ○ ○ HIGH

WHAT WAS MOST SUCCESSFUL?

WHAT COULD IMPROVE?

MEETING PLANNER

MEETING DETAILS

TIME: ....   LOCATION: ....   BADGE/JOURNEY/AWARD: ....

MEETING GOAL/THEME: ....

PRE-MEETING PREP:

SUPPLIES:
- ☐
- ☐
- ☐
- ☐
- ☐

VOLUNTEERS:
- ☐
- ☐
- ☐
- ☐
- ☐

REMINDERS:

MEETING STRUCTURE:

START-UP ACTIVITY:

OPENING:

BUSINESS:

ACTIVITIES:

(1)

(2)

(3)

(4)

(5)

CLEAN-UP & CLOSING:

NEXT MEETING:

REFLECTION:

DURING THIS MEETING, THE GIRLS...
☐ DISCOVERED ☐ CONNECTED ☐ TOOK ACTION

OUR ACTIVITIES WERE...
☐ GIRL-LED ☐ HANDS-ON ☐ COOPERATIVE

ATTENDANCE:
LOW ○ ○ ○ ○ ○ HIGH

ENJOYMENT:
LOW ○ ○ ○ ○ ○ HIGH

ENGAGEMENT:
LOW ○ ○ ○ ○ ○ HIGH

WHAT WAS MOST SUCCESSFUL?

WHAT COULD IMPROVE?

MEETING PLANNER

DATE:

MEETING DETAILS

TIME: .... LOCATION: .... BADGE/JOURNEY/AWARD: ....

MEETING GOAL/THEME: ....

PRE-MEETING PREP:

SUPPLIES:
- ☐
- ☐
- ☐
- ☐
- ☐

VOLUNTEERS:
- ☐
- ☐
- ☐
- ☐
- ☐

REMINDERS:

MEETING STRUCTURE:

START-UP ACTIVITY:

_____

OPENING:

_____

BUSINESS:

_____

ACTIVITIES:

(1)

(2)

(3)

(4)

(5)

_____

CLEAN-UP & CLOSING:

NEXT MEETING:

REFLECTION:

DURING THIS MEETING, THE GIRLS...
☐ DISCOVERED ☐ CONNECTED ☐ TOOK ACTION

OUR ACTIVITIES WERE...
☐ GIRL-LED ☐ HANDS-ON ☐ COOPERATIVE

ATTENDANCE:
LOW ○ ○ ○ ○ ○ HIGH

ENJOYMENT:
LOW ○ ○ ○ ○ ○ HIGH

ENGAGEMENT:
LOW ○ ○ ○ ○ ○ HIGH

WHAT WAS MOST SUCCESSFUL?

WHAT COULD IMPROVE?

MEETING PLANNER

DATE:

MEETING DETAILS

TIME: ....   LOCATION: ....   BADGE/JOURNEY/AWARD: ....

MEETING GOAL/THEME: ....

PRE-MEETING PREP:

SUPPLIES:
- ☐
- ☐
- ☐
- ☐
- ☐

VOLUNTEERS:
- ☐
- ☐
- ☐
- ☐
- ☐

REMINDERS:

MEETING STRUCTURE:

START-UP ACTIVITY:

OPENING:

BUSINESS:

ACTIVITIES:

(1)

(2)

(3)

(4)

(5)

CLEAN-UP & CLOSING:

NEXT MEETING:

REFLECTION:

DURING THIS MEETING, THE GIRLS...
☐ DISCOVERED ☐ CONNECTED ☐ TOOK ACTION

OUR ACTIVITIES WERE...
☐ GIRL-LED ☐ HANDS-ON ☐ COOPERATIVE

ATTENDANCE:
LOW ○ ○ ○ ○ ○ HIGH

ENJOYMENT:
LOW ○ ○ ○ ○ ○ HIGH

ENGAGEMENT:
LOW ○ ○ ○ ○ ○ HIGH

WHAT WAS MOST SUCCESSFUL?

WHAT COULD IMPROVE?

MEETING PLANNER

MEETING DETAILS

TIME: ....   LOCATION: ....   BADGE/JOURNEY/AWARD: ....

MEETING GOAL/THEME: ....

PRE-MEETING PREP:

SUPPLIES:

☐
☐
☐
☐
☐

VOLUNTEERS:

☐
☐
☐
☐
☐

REMINDERS:

MEETING STRUCTURE:

START-UP ACTIVITY:

_____

OPENING:

_____

BUSINESS:

_____

ACTIVITIES:

(1)

(2)

(3)

(4)

(5)

_____

CLEAN-UP & CLOSING:

NEXT MEETING:

REFLECTION:

DURING THIS MEETING, THE GIRLS...
☐ DISCOVERED ☐ CONNECTED ☐ TOOK ACTION

OUR ACTIVITIES WERE...
☐ GIRL-LED   ☐ HANDS-ON ☐ COOPERATIVE

ATTENDANCE:
LOW ○ ○ ○ ○ ○ HIGH

ENJOYMENT:
LOW ○ ○ ○ ○ ○ HIGH

ENGAGEMENT:
LOW ○ ○ ○ ○ ○ HIGH

WHAT WAS MOST SUCCESSFUL?

WHAT COULD IMPROVE?

MEETING PLANNER

DATE:

MEETING DETAILS

TIME: .... LOCATION: .... BADGE/JOURNEY/AWARD: ....

MEETING GOAL/THEME: ....

PRE-MEETING PREP:

SUPPLIES:
- ☐
- ☐
- ☐
- ☐
- ☐

VOLUNTEERS:
- ☐
- ☐
- ☐
- ☐
- ☐

REMINDERS:

MEETING STRUCTURE:

START-UP ACTIVITY:

OPENING:

BUSINESS:

ACTIVITIES:

(1)

(2)

(3)

(4)

(5)

CLEAN-UP & CLOSING:

NEXT MEETING:

REFLECTION:

DURING THIS MEETING, THE GIRLS...
☐ DISCOVERED ☐ CONNECTED ☐ TOOK ACTION

OUR ACTIVITIES WERE...
☐ GIRL-LED ☐ HANDS-ON ☐ COOPERATIVE

ATTENDANCE:
LOW ○ ○ ○ ○ ○ HIGH

ENJOYMENT:
LOW ○ ○ ○ ○ ○ HIGH

ENGAGEMENT:
LOW ○ ○ ○ ○ ○ HIGH

WHAT WAS MOST SUCCESSFUL?

WHAT COULD IMPROVE?

MEETING PLANNER

DATE:

MEETING DETAILS

TIME: .... LOCATION: .... BADGE/JOURNEY/AWARD: ....

MEETING GOAL/THEME: ....

PRE-MEETING PREP:

SUPPLIES:
- ☐
- ☐
- ☐
- ☐
- ☐

VOLUNTEERS:
- ☐
- ☐
- ☐
- ☐
- ☐

REMINDERS:

MEETING STRUCTURE:

START-UP ACTIVITY:

_____

OPENING:

_____

BUSINESS:

_____

ACTIVITIES:

(1)

(2)

(3)

(4)

(5)

_____

CLEAN-UP & CLOSING:

NEXT MEETING:

REFLECTION:

DURING THIS MEETING, THE GIRLS...
☐ DISCOVERED ☐ CONNECTED ☐ TOOK ACTION

OUR ACTIVITIES WERE...
☐ GIRL-LED ☐ HANDS-ON ☐ COOPERATIVE

ATTENDANCE:
LOW ○ ○ ○ ○ ○ HIGH

ENJOYMENT:
LOW ○ ○ ○ ○ ○ HIGH

ENGAGEMENT:
LOW ○ ○ ○ ○ ○ HIGH

WHAT WAS MOST SUCCESSFUL?

WHAT COULD IMPROVE?

MEETING PLANNER

DATE:

MEETING DETAILS

TIME: .... LOCATION: .... BADGE/JOURNEY/AWARD: ....

MEETING GOAL/THEME: ....

PRE-MEETING PREP:

SUPPLIES:
- ☐
- ☐
- ☐
- ☐
- ☐

VOLUNTEERS:
- ☐
- ☐
- ☐
- ☐
- ☐

REMINDERS:

MEETING STRUCTURE:

START-UP ACTIVITY:

_____

OPENING:

_____

BUSINESS:

_____

ACTIVITIES:

(1)

(2)

(3)

(4)

(5)

_____

CLEAN-UP & CLOSING:

NEXT MEETING:

REFLECTION:

DURING THIS MEETING, THE GIRLS...
☐ DISCOVERED ☐ CONNECTED ☐ TOOK ACTION

OUR ACTIVITIES WERE...
☐ GIRL-LED ☐ HANDS-ON ☐ COOPERATIVE

ATTENDANCE:
LOW ○ ○ ○ ○ ○ HIGH

ENJOYMENT:
LOW ○ ○ ○ ○ ○ HIGH

ENGAGEMENT:
LOW ○ ○ ○ ○ ○ HIGH

WHAT WAS MOST SUCCESSFUL?

WHAT COULD IMPROVE?

MEETING PLANNER

MEETING DETAILS

TIME: .... LOCATION: .... BADGE/JOURNEY/AWARD: ....

MEETING GOAL/THEME: ....

PRE-MEETING PREP:

SUPPLIES:

- [ ]
- [ ]
- [ ]
- [ ]
- [ ]

VOLUNTEERS:

- [ ]
- [ ]
- [ ]
- [ ]
- [ ]

REMINDERS:

MEETING STRUCTURE:

START-UP ACTIVITY:

_____

OPENING:

_____

BUSINESS:

_____

ACTIVITIES:

(1)

(2)

(3)

(4)

(5)

_____

CLEAN-UP & CLOSING:

NEXT MEETING:

REFLECTION:

DURING THIS MEETING, THE GIRLS...
- [ ] DISCOVERED   - [ ] CONNECTED   - [ ] TOOK ACTION

OUR ACTIVITIES WERE...
- [ ] GIRL-LED   - [ ] HANDS-ON   - [ ] COOPERATIVE

ATTENDANCE:
LOW ○ ○ ○ ○ ○ HIGH

ENJOYMENT:
LOW ○ ○ ○ ○ ○ HIGH

ENGAGEMENT:
LOW ○ ○ ○ ○ ○ HIGH

WHAT WAS MOST SUCCESSFUL?

WHAT COULD IMPROVE?

MEETING PLANNER

DATE:

MEETING DETAILS

TIME: .... LOCATION: .... BADGE/JOURNEY/AWARD: ....

MEETING GOAL/THEME: ....

PRE-MEETING PREP:

SUPPLIES:
- ☐
- ☐
- ☐
- ☐
- ☐

VOLUNTEERS:
- ☐
- ☐
- ☐
- ☐
- ☐

REMINDERS:

MEETING STRUCTURE:

START-UP ACTIVITY:

OPENING:

BUSINESS:

ACTIVITIES:

(1)

(2)

(3)

(4)

(5)

CLEAN-UP & CLOSING:

NEXT MEETING:

REFLECTION:

DURING THIS MEETING, THE GIRLS...
☐ DISCOVERED ☐ CONNECTED ☐ TOOK ACTION

OUR ACTIVITIES WERE...
☐ GIRL-LED ☐ HANDS-ON ☐ COOPERATIVE

ATTENDANCE:
LOW ○ ○ ○ ○ ○ HIGH

ENJOYMENT:
LOW ○ ○ ○ ○ ○ HIGH

ENGAGEMENT:
LOW ○ ○ ○ ○ ○ HIGH

WHAT WAS MOST SUCCESSFUL?

WHAT COULD IMPROVE?

MEETING PLANNER

DATE:

MEETING DETAILS

TIME: ....   LOCATION: ....   BADGE/JOURNEY/AWARD: ....

MEETING GOAL/THEME: ....

PRE-MEETING PREP:

SUPPLIES:

- ☐
- ☐
- ☐
- ☐
- ☐

VOLUNTEERS:

- ☐
- ☐
- ☐
- ☐
- ☐

REMINDERS:

MEETING STRUCTURE:

START-UP ACTIVITY:

_____

OPENING:

_____

BUSINESS:

_____

ACTIVITIES:

(1)

(2)

(3)

(4)

(5)

_____

CLEAN-UP & CLOSING:

NEXT MEETING:

REFLECTION:

DURING THIS MEETING, THE GIRLS...
☐ DISCOVERED ☐ CONNECTED ☐ TOOK ACTION

OUR ACTIVITIES WERE...
☐ GIRL-LED ☐ HANDS-ON ☐ COOPERATIVE

ATTENDANCE:
LOW ○ ○ ○ ○ ○ HIGH

ENJOYMENT:
LOW ○ ○ ○ ○ ○ HIGH

ENGAGEMENT:
LOW ○ ○ ○ ○ ○ HIGH

WHAT WAS MOST SUCCESSFUL?

WHAT COULD IMPROVE?

MEETING PLANNER

DATE:

MEETING DETAILS

TIME: .... LOCATION: .... BADGE/JOURNEY/AWARD: ....

MEETING GOAL/THEME: ....

PRE-MEETING PREP:

SUPPLIES:
- ☐
- ☐
- ☐
- ☐
- ☐

VOLUNTEERS:
- ☐
- ☐
- ☐
- ☐
- ☐

REMINDERS:

MEETING STRUCTURE:

START-UP ACTIVITY:

_____

OPENING:

_____

BUSINESS:

_____

ACTIVITIES:

(1)

(2)

(3)

(4)

(5)

_____

CLEAN-UP & CLOSING:

NEXT MEETING:

REFLECTION:

DURING THIS MEETING, THE GIRLS...
☐ DISCOVERED ☐ CONNECTED ☐ TOOK ACTION

OUR ACTIVITIES WERE...
☐ GIRL-LED ☐ HANDS-ON ☐ COOPERATIVE

ATTENDANCE:
LOW ○ ○ ○ ○ ○ HIGH

ENJOYMENT:
LOW ○ ○ ○ ○ ○ HIGH

ENGAGEMENT:
LOW ○ ○ ○ ○ ○ HIGH

WHAT WAS MOST SUCCESSFUL?

WHAT COULD IMPROVE?

MEETING PLANNER

DATE:

MEETING DETAILS

TIME: .... LOCATION: .... BADGE/JOURNEY/AWARD: ....

MEETING GOAL/THEME: ....

PRE-MEETING PREP:

SUPPLIES:
- ☐
- ☐
- ☐
- ☐
- ☐

VOLUNTEERS:
- ☐
- ☐
- ☐
- ☐
- ☐

REMINDERS:

MEETING STRUCTURE:

START-UP ACTIVITY:

_____

OPENING:

_____

BUSINESS:

_____

ACTIVITIES:

(1)

(2)

(3)

(4)

(5)

_____

CLEAN-UP & CLOSING:

NEXT MEETING:

REFLECTION:

DURING THIS MEETING, THE GIRLS...
☐ DISCOVERED ☐ CONNECTED ☐ TOOK ACTION

OUR ACTIVITIES WERE...
☐ GIRL-LED ☐ HANDS-ON ☐ COOPERATIVE

ATTENDANCE:
LOW ○ ○ ○ ○ ○ HIGH

ENJOYMENT:
LOW ○ ○ ○ ○ ○ HIGH

ENGAGEMENT:
LOW ○ ○ ○ ○ ○ HIGH

WHAT WAS MOST SUCCESSFUL?

WHAT COULD IMPROVE?

MEETING PLANNER

DATE:

MEETING DETAILS

TIME: ....   LOCATION: ....   BADGE/JOURNEY/AWARD: ....

MEETING GOAL/THEME: ....

PRE-MEETING PREP:

SUPPLIES:
- ☐
- ☐
- ☐
- ☐
- ☐

VOLUNTEERS:
- ☐
- ☐
- ☐
- ☐
- ☐

REMINDERS:

MEETING STRUCTURE:

START-UP ACTIVITY:

OPENING:

BUSINESS:

ACTIVITIES:

(1)

(2)

(3)

(4)

(5)

CLEAN-UP & CLOSING:

NEXT MEETING:

REFLECTION:

DURING THIS MEETING, THE GIRLS...
☐ DISCOVERED   ☐ CONNECTED   ☐ TOOK ACTION

OUR ACTIVITIES WERE...
☐ GIRL-LED   ☐ HANDS-ON   ☐ COOPERATIVE

ATTENDANCE:
LOW ○ ○ ○ ○ ○ HIGH

ENJOYMENT:
LOW ○ ○ ○ ○ ○ HIGH

ENGAGEMENT:
LOW ○ ○ ○ ○ ○ HIGH

WHAT WAS MOST SUCCESSFUL?

WHAT COULD IMPROVE?

MEETING PLANNER

DATE:

MEETING DETAILS

TIME: .... LOCATION: .... BADGE/JOURNEY/AWARD: ....

MEETING GOAL/THEME: ....

PRE-MEETING PREP:

SUPPLIES:
- ☐
- ☐
- ☐
- ☐
- ☐

VOLUNTEERS:
- ☐
- ☐
- ☐
- ☐
- ☐

REMINDERS:

MEETING STRUCTURE:

START-UP ACTIVITY:

OPENING:

BUSINESS:

ACTIVITIES:

(1)

(2)

(3)

(4)

(5)

CLEAN-UP & CLOSING:

NEXT MEETING:

REFLECTION:

DURING THIS MEETING, THE GIRLS...
☐ DISCOVERED ☐ CONNECTED ☐ TOOK ACTION

OUR ACTIVITIES WERE...
☐ GIRL-LED ☐ HANDS-ON ☐ COOPERATIVE

ATTENDANCE:
LOW ○ ○ ○ ○ ○ HIGH

ENJOYMENT:
LOW ○ ○ ○ ○ ○ HIGH

ENGAGEMENT:
LOW ○ ○ ○ ○ ○ HIGH

WHAT WAS MOST SUCCESSFUL?

WHAT COULD IMPROVE?

MEETING PLANNER

DATE:

MEETING DETAILS

TIME: .... LOCATION: .... BADGE/JOURNEY/AWARD: ....

MEETING GOAL/THEME: ....

PRE-MEETING PREP:

SUPPLIES:
- ☐
- ☐
- ☐
- ☐
- ☐

VOLUNTEERS:
- ☐
- ☐
- ☐
- ☐
- ☐

REMINDERS:

MEETING STRUCTURE:

START-UP ACTIVITY:

_____

OPENING:

_____

BUSINESS:

_____

ACTIVITIES:

(1)

(2)

(3)

(4)

(5)

_____

CLEAN-UP & CLOSING:

NEXT MEETING:

REFLECTION:

DURING THIS MEETING, THE GIRLS...
☐ DISCOVERED ☐ CONNECTED ☐ TOOK ACTION

OUR ACTIVITIES WERE...
☐ GIRL-LED   ☐ HANDS-ON ☐ COOPERATIVE

ATTENDANCE:
LOW ○ ○ ○ ○ ○ HIGH

ENJOYMENT:
LOW ○ ○ ○ ○ ○ HIGH

ENGAGEMENT:
LOW ○ ○ ○ ○ ○ HIGH

WHAT WAS MOST SUCCESSFUL?

WHAT COULD IMPROVE?

MEETING PLANNER

MEETING DETAILS

TIME: .... LOCATION: .... BADGE/JOURNEY/AWARD: ....

MEETING GOAL/THEME: ....

PRE-MEETING PREP:

SUPPLIES:
- [ ]
- [ ]
- [ ]
- [ ]
- [ ]

VOLUNTEERS:
- [ ]
- [ ]
- [ ]
- [ ]
- [ ]

REMINDERS:

MEETING STRUCTURE:

START-UP ACTIVITY:

OPENING:

BUSINESS:

ACTIVITIES:

(1)

(2)

(3)

(4)

(5)

CLEAN-UP & CLOSING:

NEXT MEETING:

REFLECTION:

DURING THIS MEETING, THE GIRLS...
- [ ] DISCOVERED [ ] CONNECTED [ ] TOOK ACTION

OUR ACTIVITIES WERE...
- [ ] GIRL-LED   [ ] HANDS-ON [ ] COOPERATIVE

ATTENDANCE:
LOW ○ ○ ○ ○ ○ HIGH

ENJOYMENT:
LOW ○ ○ ○ ○ ○ HIGH

ENGAGEMENT:
LOW ○ ○ ○ ○ ○ HIGH

WHAT WAS MOST SUCCESSFUL?

WHAT COULD IMPROVE?

MEETING PLANNER

DATE:

MEETING DETAILS

TIME: .... LOCATION: .... BADGE/JOURNEY/AWARD: ....

MEETING GOAL/THEME: ....

PRE-MEETING PREP:

SUPPLIES:
- ☐
- ☐
- ☐
- ☐
- ☐

VOLUNTEERS:
- ☐
- ☐
- ☐
- ☐
- ☐

REMINDERS:

MEETING STRUCTURE:

START-UP ACTIVITY:

_____

OPENING:

_____

BUSINESS:

_____

ACTIVITIES:

(1)

(2)

(3)

(4)

(5)

_____

CLEAN-UP & CLOSING:

NEXT MEETING:

REFLECTION:

DURING THIS MEETING, THE GIRLS...
☐ DISCOVERED ☐ CONNECTED ☐ TOOK ACTION

OUR ACTIVITIES WERE...
☐ GIRL-LED ☐ HANDS-ON ☐ COOPERATIVE

ATTENDANCE:
LOW ○ ○ ○ ○ ○ HIGH

ENJOYMENT:
LOW ○ ○ ○ ○ ○ HIGH

ENGAGEMENT:
LOW ○ ○ ○ ○ ○ HIGH

WHAT WAS MOST SUCCESSFUL?

WHAT COULD IMPROVE?

MEETING PLANNER

DATE:

MEETING DETAILS

TIME: .... LOCATION: .... BADGE/JOURNEY/AWARD: ....

MEETING GOAL/THEME: ....

PRE-MEETING PREP:

SUPPLIES:

- ☐
- ☐
- ☐
- ☐
- ☐

VOLUNTEERS:

- ☐
- ☐
- ☐
- ☐
- ☐

REMINDERS:

MEETING STRUCTURE:

START-UP ACTIVITY:

OPENING:

BUSINESS:

ACTIVITIES:

(1)

(2)

(3)

(4)

(5)

CLEAN-UP & CLOSING:

NEXT MEETING:

REFLECTION:

DURING THIS MEETING, THE GIRLS...
☐ DISCOVERED ☐ CONNECTED ☐ TOOK ACTION

OUR ACTIVITIES WERE...
☐ GIRL-LED ☐ HANDS-ON ☐ COOPERATIVE

ATTENDANCE:
LOW ○ ○ ○ ○ ○ HIGH

ENJOYMENT:
LOW ○ ○ ○ ○ ○ HIGH

ENGAGEMENT:
LOW ○ ○ ○ ○ ○ HIGH

WHAT WAS MOST SUCCESSFUL?

WHAT COULD IMPROVE?

MEETING PLANNER

DATE:

MEETING DETAILS

TIME: .... LOCATION: .... BADGE/JOURNEY/AWARD: ....

MEETING GOAL/THEME: ....

PRE-MEETING PREP:

SUPPLIES:
- ☐
- ☐
- ☐
- ☐
- ☐

VOLUNTEERS:
- ☐
- ☐
- ☐
- ☐
- ☐

REMINDERS:

MEETING STRUCTURE:

START-UP ACTIVITY:

_____

OPENING:

_____

BUSINESS:

_____

ACTIVITIES:

(1)

(2)

(3)

(4)

(5)

_____

CLEAN-UP & CLOSING:

NEXT MEETING:

REFLECTION:

DURING THIS MEETING, THE GIRLS...
☐ DISCOVERED ☐ CONNECTED ☐ TOOK ACTION

OUR ACTIVITIES WERE...
☐ GIRL-LED ☐ HANDS-ON ☐ COOPERATIVE

ATTENDANCE:
LOW ○ ○ ○ ○ ○ HIGH

ENJOYMENT:
LOW ○ ○ ○ ○ ○ HIGH

ENGAGEMENT:
LOW ○ ○ ○ ○ ○ HIGH

WHAT WAS MOST SUCCESSFUL?

WHAT COULD IMPROVE?

MEETING PLANNER

MEETING DETAILS

TIME: ....   LOCATION: ....   BADGE/JOURNEY/AWARD: ....

MEETING GOAL/THEME: ....

PRE-MEETING PREP:

SUPPLIES:
- ☐
- ☐
- ☐
- ☐
- ☐

VOLUNTEERS:
- ☐
- ☐
- ☐
- ☐
- ☐

REMINDERS:

MEETING STRUCTURE:

START-UP ACTIVITY:

_____

OPENING:

_____

BUSINESS:

_____

ACTIVITIES:

(1)

(2)

(3)

(4)

(5)

_____

CLEAN-UP & CLOSING:

NEXT MEETING:

REFLECTION:

DURING THIS MEETING, THE GIRLS...
☐ DISCOVERED ☐ CONNECTED ☐ TOOK ACTION

OUR ACTIVITIES WERE...
☐ GIRL-LED ☐ HANDS-ON ☐ COOPERATIVE

ATTENDANCE:
LOW ○ ○ ○ ○ ○ HIGH

ENJOYMENT:
LOW ○ ○ ○ ○ ○ HIGH

ENGAGEMENT:
LOW ○ ○ ○ ○ ○ HIGH

WHAT WAS MOST SUCCESSFUL?

WHAT COULD IMPROVE?

MEETING PLANNER

DATE:

MEETING DETAILS

TIME: .... LOCATION: .... BADGE/JOURNEY/AWARD: ....

MEETING GOAL/THEME: ....

PRE-MEETING PREP:

SUPPLIES:
- ☐
- ☐
- ☐
- ☐
- ☐

VOLUNTEERS:
- ☐
- ☐
- ☐
- ☐
- ☐

REMINDERS:

MEETING STRUCTURE:

START-UP ACTIVITY:

_____

OPENING:

_____

BUSINESS:

_____

ACTIVITIES:

(1)

(2)

(3)

(4)

(5)

_____

CLEAN-UP & CLOSING:

NEXT MEETING:

REFLECTION:

DURING THIS MEETING, THE GIRLS...
☐ DISCOVERED ☐ CONNECTED ☐ TOOK ACTION

OUR ACTIVITIES WERE...
☐ GIRL-LED ☐ HANDS-ON ☐ COOPERATIVE

ATTENDANCE:
LOW ○ ○ ○ ○ ○ HIGH

ENJOYMENT:
LOW ○ ○ ○ ○ ○ HIGH

ENGAGEMENT:
LOW ○ ○ ○ ○ ○ HIGH

WHAT WAS MOST SUCCESSFUL?

WHAT COULD IMPROVE?

MEETING PLANNER

DATE:

MEETING DETAILS

TIME: .... LOCATION: .... BADGE/JOURNEY/AWARD: ....

MEETING GOAL/THEME: ....

PRE-MEETING PREP:

SUPPLIES:
- ☐
- ☐
- ☐
- ☐
- ☐

VOLUNTEERS:
- ☐
- ☐
- ☐
- ☐
- ☐

REMINDERS:

MEETING STRUCTURE:

START-UP ACTIVITY:

OPENING:

BUSINESS:

ACTIVITIES:

(1)

(2)

(3)

(4)

(5)

CLEAN-UP & CLOSING:

NEXT MEETING:

REFLECTION:

DURING THIS MEETING, THE GIRLS...
☐ DISCOVERED ☐ CONNECTED ☐ TOOK ACTION

OUR ACTIVITIES WERE...
☐ GIRL-LED ☐ HANDS-ON ☐ COOPERATIVE

ATTENDANCE:
LOW ○ ○ ○ ○ ○ HIGH

ENJOYMENT:
LOW ○ ○ ○ ○ ○ HIGH

ENGAGEMENT:
LOW ○ ○ ○ ○ ○ HIGH

WHAT WAS MOST SUCCESSFUL?

WHAT COULD IMPROVE?

MEETING PLANNER

DATE:

MEETING DETAILS

TIME: .... LOCATION: .... BADGE/JOURNEY/AWARD: ....

MEETING GOAL/THEME: ....

PRE-MEETING PREP:

SUPPLIES:
- ☐
- ☐
- ☐
- ☐
- ☐

VOLUNTEERS:
- ☐
- ☐
- ☐
- ☐
- ☐

REMINDERS:

MEETING STRUCTURE:

START-UP ACTIVITY:

_____

OPENING:

_____

BUSINESS:

_____

ACTIVITIES:

(1)

(2)

(3)

(4)

(5)

_____

CLEAN-UP & CLOSING:

NEXT MEETING:

REFLECTION:

DURING THIS MEETING, THE GIRLS...
☐ DISCOVERED ☐ CONNECTED ☐ TOOK ACTION

OUR ACTIVITIES WERE...
☐ GIRL-LED ☐ HANDS-ON ☐ COOPERATIVE

ATTENDANCE:
LOW ○ ○ ○ ○ ○ HIGH

ENJOYMENT:
LOW ○ ○ ○ ○ ○ HIGH

ENGAGEMENT:
LOW ○ ○ ○ ○ ○ HIGH

WHAT WAS MOST SUCCESSFUL?

WHAT COULD IMPROVE?

MEETING PLANNER

MEETING DETAILS

TIME: .... LOCATION: .... BADGE/JOURNEY/AWARD: ....

MEETING GOAL/THEME: ....

PRE-MEETING PREP:

SUPPLIES:

- ☐
- ☐
- ☐
- ☐
- ☐

VOLUNTEERS:

- ☐
- ☐
- ☐
- ☐
- ☐

REMINDERS:

MEETING STRUCTURE:

START-UP ACTIVITY:

OPENING:

BUSINESS:

ACTIVITIES:

(1)

(2)

(3)

(4)

(5)

CLEAN-UP & CLOSING:

NEXT MEETING:

REFLECTION:

DURING THIS MEETING, THE GIRLS...
☐ DISCOVERED ☐ CONNECTED ☐ TOOK ACTION

OUR ACTIVITIES WERE...
☐ GIRL-LED ☐ HANDS-ON ☐ COOPERATIVE

ATTENDANCE:
LOW ○ ○ ○ ○ ○ HIGH

ENJOYMENT:
LOW ○ ○ ○ ○ ○ HIGH

ENGAGEMENT:
LOW ○ ○ ○ ○ ○ HIGH

WHAT WAS MOST SUCCESSFUL?

WHAT COULD IMPROVE?

MEETING PLANNER

DATE:

MEETING DETAILS

TIME: .... LOCATION: .... BADGE/JOURNEY/AWARD: ....

MEETING GOAL/THEME: ....

PRE-MEETING PREP:

SUPPLIES:
- ☐
- ☐
- ☐
- ☐
- ☐

VOLUNTEERS:
- ☐
- ☐
- ☐
- ☐
- ☐

REMINDERS:

MEETING STRUCTURE:

START-UP ACTIVITY:

OPENING:

BUSINESS:

ACTIVITIES:

(1)

(2)

(3)

(4)

(5)

CLEAN-UP & CLOSING:

NEXT MEETING:

REFLECTION:

DURING THIS MEETING, THE GIRLS...
☐ DISCOVERED ☐ CONNECTED ☐ TOOK ACTION

OUR ACTIVITIES WERE...
☐ GIRL-LED ☐ HANDS-ON ☐ COOPERATIVE

ATTENDANCE:
LOW ○ ○ ○ ○ ○ HIGH

ENJOYMENT:
LOW ○ ○ ○ ○ ○ HIGH

ENGAGEMENT:
LOW ○ ○ ○ ○ ○ HIGH

WHAT WAS MOST SUCCESSFUL?

WHAT COULD IMPROVE?

MEETING PLANNER

DATE:

MEETING DETAILS

TIME: .... LOCATION: .... BADGE/JOURNEY/AWARD: ....

MEETING GOAL/THEME: ....

PRE-MEETING PREP:

SUPPLIES:

- ☐
- ☐
- ☐
- ☐
- ☐

VOLUNTEERS:

- ☐
- ☐
- ☐
- ☐
- ☐

REMINDERS:

MEETING STRUCTURE:

START-UP ACTIVITY:

_____

OPENING:

_____

BUSINESS:

_____

ACTIVITIES:

(1)

(2)

(3)

(4)

(5)

_____

CLEAN-UP & CLOSING:

NEXT MEETING:

REFLECTION:

DURING THIS MEETING, THE GIRLS...
☐ DISCOVERED ☐ CONNECTED ☐ TOOK ACTION

OUR ACTIVITIES WERE...
☐ GIRL-LED   ☐ HANDS-ON ☐ COOPERATIVE

ATTENDANCE:
LOW ○ ○ ○ ○ ○ HIGH

ENJOYMENT:
LOW ○ ○ ○ ○ ○ HIGH

ENGAGEMENT:
LOW ○ ○ ○ ○ ○ HIGH

WHAT WAS MOST SUCCESSFUL?

WHAT COULD IMPROVE?

MEETING PLANNER

DATE:

MEETING DETAILS

TIME: .... LOCATION: .... BADGE/JOURNEY/AWARD: ....

MEETING GOAL/THEME: ....

PRE-MEETING PREP:

SUPPLIES:
- ☐
- ☐
- ☐
- ☐
- ☐

VOLUNTEERS:
- ☐
- ☐
- ☐
- ☐
- ☐

REMINDERS:

MEETING STRUCTURE:

START-UP ACTIVITY:

_____

OPENING:

_____

BUSINESS:

_____

ACTIVITIES:

(1)

(2)

(3)

(4)

(5)

_____

CLEAN-UP & CLOSING:

NEXT MEETING:

REFLECTION:

DURING THIS MEETING, THE GIRLS...
☐ DISCOVERED ☐ CONNECTED ☐ TOOK ACTION

OUR ACTIVITIES WERE...
☐ GIRL-LED ☐ HANDS-ON ☐ COOPERATIVE

ATTENDANCE:
LOW ○ ○ ○ ○ ○ HIGH

ENJOYMENT:
LOW ○ ○ ○ ○ ○ HIGH

ENGAGEMENT:
LOW ○ ○ ○ ○ ○ HIGH

WHAT WAS MOST SUCCESSFUL?

WHAT COULD IMPROVE?

MEETING PLANNER

DATE:

MEETING DETAILS

TIME: .... LOCATION: .... BADGE/JOURNEY/AWARD: ....

MEETING GOAL/THEME: ....

PRE-MEETING PREP:

SUPPLIES:

☐

☐

☐

☐

☐

VOLUNTEERS:

☐

☐

☐

☐

☐

REMINDERS:

MEETING STRUCTURE:

START-UP ACTIVITY:

_____

OPENING:

_____

BUSINESS:

_____

ACTIVITIES:

(1)

(2)

(3)

(4)

(5)

_____

CLEAN-UP & CLOSING:

NEXT MEETING:

REFLECTION:

DURING THIS MEETING, THE GIRLS...
☐ DISCOVERED ☐ CONNECTED ☐ TOOK ACTION

OUR ACTIVITIES WERE...
☐ GIRL-LED ☐ HANDS-ON ☐ COOPERATIVE

ATTENDANCE:
LOW ○ ○ ○ ○ ○ HIGH

ENJOYMENT:
LOW ○ ○ ○ ○ ○ HIGH

ENGAGEMENT:
LOW ○ ○ ○ ○ ○ HIGH

WHAT WAS MOST SUCCESSFUL?

WHAT COULD IMPROVE?

MEETING PLANNER

DATE:

MEETING DETAILS

TIME: .... LOCATION: .... BADGE/JOURNEY/AWARD: ....

MEETING GOAL/THEME: ....

PRE-MEETING PREP:

SUPPLIES:
- ☐
- ☐
- ☐
- ☐
- ☐

VOLUNTEERS:
- ☐
- ☐
- ☐
- ☐
- ☐

REMINDERS:

MEETING STRUCTURE:

START-UP ACTIVITY:

OPENING:

BUSINESS:

ACTIVITIES:

(1)

(2)

(3)

(4)

(5)

CLEAN-UP & CLOSING:

NEXT MEETING:

REFLECTION:

DURING THIS MEETING, THE GIRLS...
☐ DISCOVERED ☐ CONNECTED ☐ TOOK ACTION

OUR ACTIVITIES WERE...
☐ GIRL-LED ☐ HANDS-ON ☐ COOPERATIVE

ATTENDANCE:
LOW ○ ○ ○ ○ ○ HIGH

ENJOYMENT:
LOW ○ ○ ○ ○ ○ HIGH

ENGAGEMENT:
LOW ○ ○ ○ ○ ○ HIGH

WHAT WAS MOST SUCCESSFUL?

WHAT COULD IMPROVE?

MEETING PLANNER

DATE: ....

MEETING DETAILS

TIME: ....   LOCATION: ....   BADGE/JOURNEY/AWARD: ....

MEETING GOAL/THEME: ....

PRE-MEETING PREP:

SUPPLIES:
- ☐
- ☐
- ☐
- ☐
- ☐

VOLUNTEERS:
- ☐
- ☐
- ☐
- ☐
- ☐

REMINDERS:

MEETING STRUCTURE:

START-UP ACTIVITY:

_____

OPENING:

_____

BUSINESS:

_____

ACTIVITIES:

(1)

(2)

(3)

(4)

(5)

_____

CLEAN-UP & CLOSING:

NEXT MEETING:

REFLECTION:

DURING THIS MEETING, THE GIRLS...
☐ DISCOVERED ☐ CONNECTED ☐ TOOK ACTION

OUR ACTIVITIES WERE...
☐ GIRL-LED   ☐ HANDS-ON ☐ COOPERATIVE

ATTENDANCE:
LOW ○ ○ ○ ○ ○ HIGH

ENJOYMENT:
LOW ○ ○ ○ ○ ○ HIGH

ENGAGEMENT:
LOW ○ ○ ○ ○ ○ HIGH

WHAT WAS MOST SUCCESSFUL?

WHAT COULD IMPROVE?

MEETING PLANNER

DATE:

MEETING DETAILS

TIME: .... LOCATION: .... BADGE/JOURNEY/AWARD: ....

MEETING GOAL/THEME: ....

PRE-MEETING PREP:

SUPPLIES:
- ☐
- ☐
- ☐
- ☐
- ☐

VOLUNTEERS:
- ☐
- ☐
- ☐
- ☐
- ☐

REMINDERS:

MEETING STRUCTURE:

START-UP ACTIVITY:

_____

OPENING:

_____

BUSINESS:

_____

ACTIVITIES:

(1)

(2)

(3)

(4)

(5)

_____

CLEAN-UP & CLOSING:

NEXT MEETING:

REFLECTION:

DURING THIS MEETING, THE GIRLS...
☐ DISCOVERED ☐ CONNECTED ☐ TOOK ACTION

OUR ACTIVITIES WERE...
☐ GIRL-LED ☐ HANDS-ON ☐ COOPERATIVE

ATTENDANCE:
LOW ○ ○ ○ ○ ○ HIGH

ENJOYMENT:
LOW ○ ○ ○ ○ ○ HIGH

ENGAGEMENT:
LOW ○ ○ ○ ○ ○ HIGH

WHAT WAS MOST SUCCESSFUL?

WHAT COULD IMPROVE?

MEETING PLANNER

MEETING DETAILS

TIME: .... LOCATION: .... BADGE/JOURNEY/AWARD: ....

MEETING GOAL/THEME: ....

PRE-MEETING PREP:

SUPPLIES:
- ☐
- ☐
- ☐
- ☐
- ☐

VOLUNTEERS:
- ☐
- ☐
- ☐
- ☐
- ☐

REMINDERS:

MEETING STRUCTURE:

START-UP ACTIVITY:

_____

OPENING:

_____

BUSINESS:

_____

ACTIVITIES:

(1)

(2)

(3)

(4)

(5)

_____

CLEAN-UP & CLOSING:

NEXT MEETING:

REFLECTION:

DURING THIS MEETING, THE GIRLS...
☐ DISCOVERED ☐ CONNECTED ☐ TOOK ACTION

OUR ACTIVITIES WERE...
☐ GIRL-LED   ☐ HANDS-ON ☐ COOPERATIVE

ATTENDANCE:
LOW ○ ○ ○ ○ ○ HIGH

ENJOYMENT:
LOW ○ ○ ○ ○ ○ HIGH

ENGAGEMENT:
LOW ○ ○ ○ ○ ○ HIGH

WHAT WAS MOST SUCCESSFUL?

WHAT COULD IMPROVE?

MEETING PLANNER

DATE:

MEETING DETAILS

TIME: .... LOCATION: .... BADGE/JOURNEY/AWARD: ....

MEETING GOAL/THEME: ....

PRE-MEETING PREP:

SUPPLIES:
- ☐
- ☐
- ☐
- ☐
- ☐

VOLUNTEERS:
- ☐
- ☐
- ☐
- ☐
- ☐

REMINDERS:

MEETING STRUCTURE:

START-UP ACTIVITY:

_____

OPENING:

_____

BUSINESS:

_____

ACTIVITIES:

(1)

(2)

(3)

(4)

(5)

_____

CLEAN-UP & CLOSING:

NEXT MEETING:

REFLECTION:

DURING THIS MEETING, THE GIRLS...
☐ DISCOVERED ☐ CONNECTED ☐ TOOK ACTION

OUR ACTIVITIES WERE...
☐ GIRL-LED ☐ HANDS-ON ☐ COOPERATIVE

ATTENDANCE:
LOW ○ ○ ○ ○ ○ HIGH

ENJOYMENT:
LOW ○ ○ ○ ○ ○ HIGH

ENGAGEMENT:
LOW ○ ○ ○ ○ ○ HIGH

WHAT WAS MOST SUCCESSFUL?

WHAT COULD IMPROVE?

BADGE ACTIVITIES PLANNER

BADGE: ....

PURPOSE: ....

\# OF MEETINGS TO COMPLETE THIS BADGE: .... JOURNEY CONNECTION(S): .... ☐ STEP 1 ☐ STEP 2 ☐ STEP 3 ☐ STEP 4 ☐ STEP 5

LONG-TERM PLANNING:

FIELD TRIP/GUEST SPEAKER IDEAS:

STEP 1:
TIME NEEDED: .... MINUTES

ACTIVITY: .... TO BE COMPLETED AT: ☐ HOME ☐ MEETING ☐ EVENT ☐ FIELD TRIP

PREP/SUPPLIES NEEDED:
WHO'S RESPONSIBLE?

(1) .... ☐ LEADER ☐ GIRL/VOLUNTEER: ....

(2) .... ☐ LEADER ☐ GIRL/VOLUNTEER: ....

(3) .... ☐ LEADER ☐ GIRL/VOLUNTEER: ....

(4) .... ☐ LEADER ☐ GIRL/VOLUNTEER: ....

(5) .... ☐ LEADER ☐ GIRL/VOLUNTEER: ....

ACTIVITY STEPS/NOTES:

LEADERSHIP KEYS: ☐ DISCOVER ☐ CONNECT ☐ TAKE ACTION   PROCESSES: ☐ GIRL-LED ☐ LEARNING BY DOING ☐ COOPERATIVE LEARNING

STEP 2:
TIME NEEDED: .... MINUTES

ACTIVITY: .... TO BE COMPLETED AT: ☐ HOME ☐ MEETING ☐ EVENT ☐ FIELD TRIP

PREP/SUPPLIES NEEDED:
WHO'S RESPONSIBLE?

(1) .... ☐ LEADER ☐ GIRL/VOLUNTEER: ....

(2) .... ☐ LEADER ☐ GIRL/VOLUNTEER: ....

(3) .... ☐ LEADER ☐ GIRL/VOLUNTEER: ....

(4) .... ☐ LEADER ☐ GIRL/VOLUNTEER: ....

(5) .... ☐ LEADER ☐ GIRL/VOLUNTEER: ....

ACTIVITY STEPS/NOTES:

LEADERSHIP KEYS: ☐ DISCOVER ☐ CONNECT ☐ TAKE ACTION   PROCESSES: ☐ GIRL-LED ☐ LEARNING BY DOING ☐ COOPERATIVE LEARNING

STEP 3:

TIME NEEDED: .... MINUTES

ACTIVITY: .... TO BE COMPLETED AT: ☐ HOME ☐ MEETING ☐ EVENT ☐ FIELD TRIP

PREP/SUPPLIES NEEDED:

WHO'S RESPONSIBLE?

(1) .... ☐ LEADER ☐ GIRL/VOLUNTEER: ....

(2) .... ☐ LEADER ☐ GIRL/VOLUNTEER: ....

(3) .... ☐ LEADER ☐ GIRL/VOLUNTEER: ....

(4) .... ☐ LEADER ☐ GIRL/VOLUNTEER: ....

(5) .... ☐ LEADER ☐ GIRL/VOLUNTEER: ....

ACTIVITY STEPS/NOTES:

LEADERSHIP KEYS: ☐ DISCOVER ☐ CONNECT ☐ TAKE ACTION   PROCESSES: ☐ GIRL-LED ☐ LEARNING BY DOING ☐ COOPERATIVE LEARNING

STEP 4:

TIME NEEDED: .... MINUTES

ACTIVITY: .... TO BE COMPLETED AT: ☐ HOME ☐ MEETING ☐ EVENT ☐ FIELD TRIP

PREP/SUPPLIES NEEDED:

WHO'S RESPONSIBLE?

(1) .... ☐ LEADER ☐ GIRL/VOLUNTEER: ....

(2) .... ☐ LEADER ☐ GIRL/VOLUNTEER: ....

(3) .... ☐ LEADER ☐ GIRL/VOLUNTEER: ....

(4) .... ☐ LEADER ☐ GIRL/VOLUNTEER: ....

(5) .... ☐ LEADER ☐ GIRL/VOLUNTEER: ....

ACTIVITY STEPS/NOTES:

LEADERSHIP KEYS: ☐ DISCOVER ☐ CONNECT ☐ TAKE ACTION   PROCESSES: ☐ GIRL-LED ☐ LEARNING BY DOING ☐ COOPERATIVE LEARNING

STEP 5:

TIME NEEDED: .... MINUTES

ACTIVITY: .... TO BE COMPLETED AT: ☐ HOME ☐ MEETING ☐ EVENT ☐ FIELD TRIP

PREP/SUPPLIES NEEDED:

WHO'S RESPONSIBLE?

(1) .... ☐ LEADER ☐ GIRL/VOLUNTEER: ....

(2) .... ☐ LEADER ☐ GIRL/VOLUNTEER: ....

(3) .... ☐ LEADER ☐ GIRL/VOLUNTEER: ....

(4) .... ☐ LEADER ☐ GIRL/VOLUNTEER: ....

(5) .... ☐ LEADER ☐ GIRL/VOLUNTEER: ....

ACTIVITY STEPS/NOTES:

LEADERSHIP KEYS: ☐ DISCOVER ☐ CONNECT ☐ TAKE ACTION   PROCESSES: ☐ GIRL-LED ☐ LEARNING BY DOING ☐ COOPERATIVE LEARNING

BADGE ACTIVITIES PLANNER

BADGE:

PURPOSE: ....

OF MEETINGS TO COMPLETE THIS BADGE: .... JOURNEY CONNECTION(S): .... ☐ STEP 1 ☐ STEP 2 ☐ STEP 3 ☐ STEP 4 ☐ STEP 5

LONG-TERM PLANNING:

FIELD TRIP/GUEST SPEAKER IDEAS:

STEP 1:   TIME NEEDED: .... MINUTES

ACTIVITY: .... TO BE COMPLETED AT: ☐ HOME ☐ MEETING ☐ EVENT ☐ FIELD TRIP

PREP/SUPPLIES NEEDED: WHO'S RESPONSIBLE?

(1) .... ☐ LEADER ☐ GIRL/VOLUNTEER: ....

(2) .... ☐ LEADER ☐ GIRL/VOLUNTEER: ....

(3) .... ☐ LEADER ☐ GIRL/VOLUNTEER: ....

(4) .... ☐ LEADER ☐ GIRL/VOLUNTEER: ....

(5) .... ☐ LEADER ☐ GIRL/VOLUNTEER: ....

ACTIVITY STEPS/NOTES:

LEADERSHIP KEYS: ☐ DISCOVER ☐ CONNECT ☐ TAKE ACTION   PROCESSES: ☐ GIRL-LED ☐ LEARNING BY DOING ☐ COOPERATIVE LEARNING

STEP 2:   TIME NEEDED: .... MINUTES

ACTIVITY: .... TO BE COMPLETED AT: ☐ HOME ☐ MEETING ☐ EVENT ☐ FIELD TRIP

PREP/SUPPLIES NEEDED: WHO'S RESPONSIBLE?

(1) .... ☐ LEADER ☐ GIRL/VOLUNTEER: ....

(2) .... ☐ LEADER ☐ GIRL/VOLUNTEER: ....

(3) .... ☐ LEADER ☐ GIRL/VOLUNTEER: ....

(4) .... ☐ LEADER ☐ GIRL/VOLUNTEER: ....

(5) .... ☐ LEADER ☐ GIRL/VOLUNTEER: ....

ACTIVITY STEPS/NOTES:

LEADERSHIP KEYS: ☐ DISCOVER ☐ CONNECT ☐ TAKE ACTION   PROCESSES: ☐ GIRL-LED ☐ LEARNING BY DOING ☐ COOPERATIVE LEARNING

STEP 3:

TIME NEEDED: .... MINUTES

ACTIVITY: .... TO BE COMPLETED AT: ☐ HOME ☐ MEETING ☐ EVENT ☐ FIELD TRIP

PREP/SUPPLIES NEEDED:

WHO'S RESPONSIBLE?

(1) .... ☐ LEADER ☐ GIRL/VOLUNTEER: ....

(2) .... ☐ LEADER ☐ GIRL/VOLUNTEER: ....

(3) .... ☐ LEADER ☐ GIRL/VOLUNTEER: ....

(4) .... ☐ LEADER ☐ GIRL/VOLUNTEER: ....

(5) .... ☐ LEADER ☐ GIRL/VOLUNTEER: ....

ACTIVITY STEPS/NOTES:

LEADERSHIP KEYS: ☐ DISCOVER ☐ CONNECT ☐ TAKE ACTION   PROCESSES: ☐ GIRL-LED ☐ LEARNING BY DOING ☐ COOPERATIVE LEARNING

STEP 4:

TIME NEEDED: .... MINUTES

ACTIVITY: .... TO BE COMPLETED AT: ☐ HOME ☐ MEETING ☐ EVENT ☐ FIELD TRIP

PREP/SUPPLIES NEEDED:

WHO'S RESPONSIBLE?

(1) .... ☐ LEADER ☐ GIRL/VOLUNTEER: ....

(2) .... ☐ LEADER ☐ GIRL/VOLUNTEER: ....

(3) .... ☐ LEADER ☐ GIRL/VOLUNTEER: ....

(4) .... ☐ LEADER ☐ GIRL/VOLUNTEER: ....

(5) .... ☐ LEADER ☐ GIRL/VOLUNTEER: ....

ACTIVITY STEPS/NOTES:

LEADERSHIP KEYS: ☐ DISCOVER ☐ CONNECT ☐ TAKE ACTION   PROCESSES: ☐ GIRL-LED ☐ LEARNING BY DOING ☐ COOPERATIVE LEARNING

STEP 5:

TIME NEEDED: .... MINUTES

ACTIVITY: .... TO BE COMPLETED AT: ☐ HOME ☐ MEETING ☐ EVENT ☐ FIELD TRIP

PREP/SUPPLIES NEEDED:

WHO'S RESPONSIBLE?

(1) .... ☐ LEADER ☐ GIRL/VOLUNTEER: ....

(2) .... ☐ LEADER ☐ GIRL/VOLUNTEER: ....

(3) .... ☐ LEADER ☐ GIRL/VOLUNTEER: ....

(4) .... ☐ LEADER ☐ GIRL/VOLUNTEER: ....

(5) .... ☐ LEADER ☐ GIRL/VOLUNTEER: ....

ACTIVITY STEPS/NOTES:

LEADERSHIP KEYS: ☐ DISCOVER ☐ CONNECT ☐ TAKE ACTION   PROCESSES: ☐ GIRL-LED ☐ LEARNING BY DOING ☐ COOPERATIVE LEARNING

BADGE ACTIVITIES PLANNER

BADGE: ....

PURPOSE: ....

\# OF MEETINGS TO COMPLETE THIS BADGE: .... JOURNEY CONNECTION(S): ....   ☐ STEP 1 ☐ STEP 2 ☐ STEP 3 ☐ STEP 4 ☐ STEP 5

LONG-TERM PLANNING:

FIELD TRIP/GUEST SPEAKER IDEAS:

STEP 1:   TIME NEEDED: .... MINUTES

ACTIVITY: .... TO BE COMPLETED AT: ☐ HOME ☐ MEETING ☐ EVENT ☐ FIELD TRIP

PREP/SUPPLIES NEEDED: WHO'S RESPONSIBLE?

(1) .... ☐ LEADER ☐ GIRL/VOLUNTEER: ....

(2) .... ☐ LEADER ☐ GIRL/VOLUNTEER: ....

(3) .... ☐ LEADER ☐ GIRL/VOLUNTEER: ....

(4) .... ☐ LEADER ☐ GIRL/VOLUNTEER: ....

(5) .... ☐ LEADER ☐ GIRL/VOLUNTEER: ....

ACTIVITY STEPS/NOTES:

LEADERSHIP KEYS: ☐ DISCOVER ☐ CONNECT ☐ TAKE ACTION   PROCESSES: ☐ GIRL-LED ☐ LEARNING BY DOING ☐ COOPERATIVE LEARNING

STEP 2:   TIME NEEDED: .... MINUTES

ACTIVITY: .... TO BE COMPLETED AT: ☐ HOME ☐ MEETING ☐ EVENT ☐ FIELD TRIP

PREP/SUPPLIES NEEDED: WHO'S RESPONSIBLE?

(1) .... ☐ LEADER ☐ GIRL/VOLUNTEER: ....

(2) .... ☐ LEADER ☐ GIRL/VOLUNTEER: ....

(3) .... ☐ LEADER ☐ GIRL/VOLUNTEER: ....

(4) .... ☐ LEADER ☐ GIRL/VOLUNTEER: ....

(5) .... ☐ LEADER ☐ GIRL/VOLUNTEER: ....

ACTIVITY STEPS/NOTES:

LEADERSHIP KEYS: ☐ DISCOVER ☐ CONNECT ☐ TAKE ACTION   PROCESSES: ☐ GIRL-LED ☐ LEARNING BY DOING ☐ COOPERATIVE LEARNING

STEP 3:

TIME NEEDED: .... MINUTES

ACTIVITY: .... TO BE COMPLETED AT: ☐ HOME ☐ MEETING ☐ EVENT ☐ FIELD TRIP

PREP/SUPPLIES NEEDED:

WHO'S RESPONSIBLE?

(1) .... ☐ LEADER ☐ GIRL/VOLUNTEER: ....

(2) .... ☐ LEADER ☐ GIRL/VOLUNTEER: ....

(3) .... ☐ LEADER ☐ GIRL/VOLUNTEER: ....

(4) .... ☐ LEADER ☐ GIRL/VOLUNTEER: ....

(5) .... ☐ LEADER ☐ GIRL/VOLUNTEER: ....

ACTIVITY STEPS/NOTES:

LEADERSHIP KEYS: ☐ DISCOVER ☐ CONNECT ☐ TAKE ACTION   PROCESSES: ☐ GIRL-LED ☐ LEARNING BY DOING ☐ COOPERATIVE LEARNING

STEP 4:

TIME NEEDED: .... MINUTES

ACTIVITY: .... TO BE COMPLETED AT: ☐ HOME ☐ MEETING ☐ EVENT ☐ FIELD TRIP

PREP/SUPPLIES NEEDED:

WHO'S RESPONSIBLE?

(1) .... ☐ LEADER ☐ GIRL/VOLUNTEER: ....

(2) .... ☐ LEADER ☐ GIRL/VOLUNTEER: ....

(3) .... ☐ LEADER ☐ GIRL/VOLUNTEER: ....

(4) .... ☐ LEADER ☐ GIRL/VOLUNTEER: ....

(5) .... ☐ LEADER ☐ GIRL/VOLUNTEER: ....

ACTIVITY STEPS/NOTES:

LEADERSHIP KEYS: ☐ DISCOVER ☐ CONNECT ☐ TAKE ACTION   PROCESSES: ☐ GIRL-LED ☐ LEARNING BY DOING ☐ COOPERATIVE LEARNING

STEP 5:

TIME NEEDED: .... MINUTES

ACTIVITY: .... TO BE COMPLETED AT: ☐ HOME ☐ MEETING ☐ EVENT ☐ FIELD TRIP

PREP/SUPPLIES NEEDED:

WHO'S RESPONSIBLE?

(1) .... ☐ LEADER ☐ GIRL/VOLUNTEER: ....

(2) .... ☐ LEADER ☐ GIRL/VOLUNTEER: ....

(3) .... ☐ LEADER ☐ GIRL/VOLUNTEER: ....

(4) .... ☐ LEADER ☐ GIRL/VOLUNTEER: ....

(5) .... ☐ LEADER ☐ GIRL/VOLUNTEER: ....

ACTIVITY STEPS/NOTES:

LEADERSHIP KEYS: ☐ DISCOVER ☐ CONNECT ☐ TAKE ACTION   PROCESSES: ☐ GIRL-LED ☐ LEARNING BY DOING ☐ COOPERATIVE LEARNING

BADGE ACTIVITIES PLANNER

BADGE:

PURPOSE: ....

OF MEETINGS TO COMPLETE THIS BADGE: .... JOURNEY CONNECTION(S): .... ☐ STEP 1 ☐ STEP 2 ☐ STEP 3 ☐ STEP 4 ☐ STEP 5

LONG-TERM PLANNING:

FIELD TRIP/GUEST SPEAKER IDEAS:

STEP 1:   TIME NEEDED: .... MINUTES

ACTIVITY: .... TO BE COMPLETED AT: ☐ HOME ☐ MEETING ☐ EVENT ☐ FIELD TRIP

PREP/SUPPLIES NEEDED: WHO'S RESPONSIBLE?

(1) .... ☐ LEADER ☐ GIRL/VOLUNTEER: ....

(2) .... ☐ LEADER ☐ GIRL/VOLUNTEER: ....

(3) .... ☐ LEADER ☐ GIRL/VOLUNTEER: ....

(4) .... ☐ LEADER ☐ GIRL/VOLUNTEER: ....

(5) .... ☐ LEADER ☐ GIRL/VOLUNTEER: ....

ACTIVITY STEPS/NOTES:

LEADERSHIP KEYS: ☐ DISCOVER ☐ CONNECT ☐ TAKE ACTION   PROCESSES: ☐ GIRL-LED ☐ LEARNING BY DOING ☐ COOPERATIVE LEARNING

STEP 2:   TIME NEEDED: .... MINUTES

ACTIVITY: .... TO BE COMPLETED AT: ☐ HOME ☐ MEETING ☐ EVENT ☐ FIELD TRIP

PREP/SUPPLIES NEEDED: WHO'S RESPONSIBLE?

(1) .... ☐ LEADER ☐ GIRL/VOLUNTEER: ....

(2) .... ☐ LEADER ☐ GIRL/VOLUNTEER: ....

(3) .... ☐ LEADER ☐ GIRL/VOLUNTEER: ....

(4) .... ☐ LEADER ☐ GIRL/VOLUNTEER: ....

(5) .... ☐ LEADER ☐ GIRL/VOLUNTEER: ....

ACTIVITY STEPS/NOTES:

LEADERSHIP KEYS: ☐ DISCOVER ☐ CONNECT ☐ TAKE ACTION   PROCESSES: ☐ GIRL-LED ☐ LEARNING BY DOING ☐ COOPERATIVE LEARNING

STEP 3:

TIME NEEDED: .... MINUTES

ACTIVITY: .... TO BE COMPLETED AT: ☐ HOME ☐ MEETING ☐ EVENT ☐ FIELD TRIP

PREP/SUPPLIES NEEDED:

WHO'S RESPONSIBLE?

(1) .... ☐ LEADER ☐ GIRL/VOLUNTEER: ....

(2) .... ☐ LEADER ☐ GIRL/VOLUNTEER: ....

(3) .... ☐ LEADER ☐ GIRL/VOLUNTEER: ....

(4) .... ☐ LEADER ☐ GIRL/VOLUNTEER: ....

(5) .... ☐ LEADER ☐ GIRL/VOLUNTEER: ....

ACTIVITY STEPS/NOTES:

LEADERSHIP KEYS: ☐ DISCOVER ☐ CONNECT ☐ TAKE ACTION   PROCESSES: ☐ GIRL-LED ☐ LEARNING BY DOING ☐ COOPERATIVE LEARNING

STEP 4:

TIME NEEDED: .... MINUTES

ACTIVITY: .... TO BE COMPLETED AT: ☐ HOME ☐ MEETING ☐ EVENT ☐ FIELD TRIP

PREP/SUPPLIES NEEDED:

WHO'S RESPONSIBLE?

(1) .... ☐ LEADER ☐ GIRL/VOLUNTEER: ....

(2) .... ☐ LEADER ☐ GIRL/VOLUNTEER: ....

(3) .... ☐ LEADER ☐ GIRL/VOLUNTEER: ....

(4) .... ☐ LEADER ☐ GIRL/VOLUNTEER: ....

(5) .... ☐ LEADER ☐ GIRL/VOLUNTEER: ....

ACTIVITY STEPS/NOTES:

LEADERSHIP KEYS: ☐ DISCOVER ☐ CONNECT ☐ TAKE ACTION   PROCESSES: ☐ GIRL-LED ☐ LEARNING BY DOING ☐ COOPERATIVE LEARNING

STEP 5:

TIME NEEDED: .... MINUTES

ACTIVITY: .... TO BE COMPLETED AT: ☐ HOME ☐ MEETING ☐ EVENT ☐ FIELD TRIP

PREP/SUPPLIES NEEDED:

WHO'S RESPONSIBLE?

(1) .... ☐ LEADER ☐ GIRL/VOLUNTEER: ....

(2) .... ☐ LEADER ☐ GIRL/VOLUNTEER: ....

(3) .... ☐ LEADER ☐ GIRL/VOLUNTEER: ....

(4) .... ☐ LEADER ☐ GIRL/VOLUNTEER: ....

(5) .... ☐ LEADER ☐ GIRL/VOLUNTEER: ....

ACTIVITY STEPS/NOTES:

LEADERSHIP KEYS: ☐ DISCOVER ☐ CONNECT ☐ TAKE ACTION   PROCESSES: ☐ GIRL-LED ☐ LEARNING BY DOING ☐ COOPERATIVE LEARNING

BADGE ACTIVITIES PLANNER

BADGE:

PURPOSE: ....

OF MEETINGS TO COMPLETE THIS BADGE: .... JOURNEY CONNECTION(S): .... ☐ STEP 1 ☐ STEP 2 ☐ STEP 3 ☐ STEP 4 ☐ STEP 5

LONG-TERM PLANNING:

FIELD TRIP/GUEST SPEAKER IDEAS:

STEP 1:   TIME NEEDED: .... MINUTES

ACTIVITY: .... TO BE COMPLETED AT: ☐ HOME ☐ MEETING ☐ EVENT ☐ FIELD TRIP

PREP/SUPPLIES NEEDED: WHO'S RESPONSIBLE?

(1) .... ☐ LEADER ☐ GIRL/VOLUNTEER: ....

(2) .... ☐ LEADER ☐ GIRL/VOLUNTEER: ....

(3) .... ☐ LEADER ☐ GIRL/VOLUNTEER: ....

(4) .... ☐ LEADER ☐ GIRL/VOLUNTEER: ....

(5) .... ☐ LEADER ☐ GIRL/VOLUNTEER: ....

ACTIVITY STEPS/NOTES:

LEADERSHIP KEYS: ☐ DISCOVER ☐ CONNECT ☐ TAKE ACTION   PROCESSES: ☐ GIRL-LED ☐ LEARNING BY DOING ☐ COOPERATIVE LEARNING

STEP 2:   TIME NEEDED: .... MINUTES

ACTIVITY: .... TO BE COMPLETED AT: ☐ HOME ☐ MEETING ☐ EVENT ☐ FIELD TRIP

PREP/SUPPLIES NEEDED: WHO'S RESPONSIBLE?

(1) .... ☐ LEADER ☐ GIRL/VOLUNTEER: ....

(2) .... ☐ LEADER ☐ GIRL/VOLUNTEER: ....

(3) .... ☐ LEADER ☐ GIRL/VOLUNTEER: ....

(4) .... ☐ LEADER ☐ GIRL/VOLUNTEER: ....

(5) .... ☐ LEADER ☐ GIRL/VOLUNTEER: ....

ACTIVITY STEPS/NOTES:

LEADERSHIP KEYS: ☐ DISCOVER ☐ CONNECT ☐ TAKE ACTION   PROCESSES: ☐ GIRL-LED ☐ LEARNING BY DOING ☐ COOPERATIVE LEARNING

STEP 3:

TIME NEEDED: .... MINUTES

ACTIVITY: .... TO BE COMPLETED AT: ☐ HOME ☐ MEETING ☐ EVENT ☐ FIELD TRIP

PREP/SUPPLIES NEEDED:

WHO'S RESPONSIBLE?

(1) .... ☐ LEADER ☐ GIRL/VOLUNTEER: ....

(2) .... ☐ LEADER ☐ GIRL/VOLUNTEER: ....

(3) .... ☐ LEADER ☐ GIRL/VOLUNTEER: ....

(4) .... ☐ LEADER ☐ GIRL/VOLUNTEER: ....

(5) .... ☐ LEADER ☐ GIRL/VOLUNTEER: ....

ACTIVITY STEPS/NOTES:

LEADERSHIP KEYS: ☐ DISCOVER ☐ CONNECT ☐ TAKE ACTION   PROCESSES: ☐ GIRL-LED ☐ LEARNING BY DOING ☐ COOPERATIVE LEARNING

STEP 4:

TIME NEEDED: .... MINUTES

ACTIVITY: .... TO BE COMPLETED AT: ☐ HOME ☐ MEETING ☐ EVENT ☐ FIELD TRIP

PREP/SUPPLIES NEEDED:

WHO'S RESPONSIBLE?

(1) .... ☐ LEADER ☐ GIRL/VOLUNTEER: ....

(2) .... ☐ LEADER ☐ GIRL/VOLUNTEER: ....

(3) .... ☐ LEADER ☐ GIRL/VOLUNTEER: ....

(4) .... ☐ LEADER ☐ GIRL/VOLUNTEER: ....

(5) .... ☐ LEADER ☐ GIRL/VOLUNTEER: ....

ACTIVITY STEPS/NOTES:

LEADERSHIP KEYS: ☐ DISCOVER ☐ CONNECT ☐ TAKE ACTION   PROCESSES: ☐ GIRL-LED ☐ LEARNING BY DOING ☐ COOPERATIVE LEARNING

STEP 5:

TIME NEEDED: .... MINUTES

ACTIVITY: .... TO BE COMPLETED AT: ☐ HOME ☐ MEETING ☐ EVENT ☐ FIELD TRIP

PREP/SUPPLIES NEEDED:

WHO'S RESPONSIBLE?

(1) .... ☐ LEADER ☐ GIRL/VOLUNTEER: ....

(2) .... ☐ LEADER ☐ GIRL/VOLUNTEER: ....

(3) .... ☐ LEADER ☐ GIRL/VOLUNTEER: ....

(4) .... ☐ LEADER ☐ GIRL/VOLUNTEER: ....

(5) .... ☐ LEADER ☐ GIRL/VOLUNTEER: ....

ACTIVITY STEPS/NOTES:

LEADERSHIP KEYS: ☐ DISCOVER ☐ CONNECT ☐ TAKE ACTION   PROCESSES: ☐ GIRL-LED ☐ LEARNING BY DOING ☐ COOPERATIVE LEARNING

BADGE ACTIVITIES PLANNER

BADGE:

PURPOSE: ....

OF MEETINGS TO COMPLETE THIS BADGE: .... JOURNEY CONNECTION(S): .... ☐ STEP 1 ☐ STEP 2 ☐ STEP 3 ☐ STEP 4 ☐ STEP 5

LONG-TERM PLANNING:

FIELD TRIP/GUEST SPEAKER IDEAS:

STEP 1:
TIME NEEDED: .... MINUTES

ACTIVITY: .... TO BE COMPLETED AT: ☐ HOME ☐ MEETING ☐ EVENT ☐ FIELD TRIP

PREP/SUPPLIES NEEDED: WHO'S RESPONSIBLE?

(1) .... ☐ LEADER ☐ GIRL/VOLUNTEER: ....

(2) .... ☐ LEADER ☐ GIRL/VOLUNTEER: ....

(3) .... ☐ LEADER ☐ GIRL/VOLUNTEER: ....

(4) .... ☐ LEADER ☐ GIRL/VOLUNTEER: ....

(5) .... ☐ LEADER ☐ GIRL/VOLUNTEER: ....

ACTIVITY STEPS/NOTES:

LEADERSHIP KEYS: ☐ DISCOVER ☐ CONNECT ☐ TAKE ACTION   PROCESSES: ☐ GIRL-LED ☐ LEARNING BY DOING ☐ COOPERATIVE LEARNING

STEP 2:
TIME NEEDED: .... MINUTES

ACTIVITY: .... TO BE COMPLETED AT: ☐ HOME ☐ MEETING ☐ EVENT ☐ FIELD TRIP

PREP/SUPPLIES NEEDED: WHO'S RESPONSIBLE?

(1) .... ☐ LEADER ☐ GIRL/VOLUNTEER: ....

(2) .... ☐ LEADER ☐ GIRL/VOLUNTEER: ....

(3) .... ☐ LEADER ☐ GIRL/VOLUNTEER: ....

(4) .... ☐ LEADER ☐ GIRL/VOLUNTEER: ....

(5) .... ☐ LEADER ☐ GIRL/VOLUNTEER: ....

ACTIVITY STEPS/NOTES:

LEADERSHIP KEYS: ☐ DISCOVER ☐ CONNECT ☐ TAKE ACTION   PROCESSES: ☐ GIRL-LED ☐ LEARNING BY DOING ☐ COOPERATIVE LEARNING

STEP 3:

TIME NEEDED: .... MINUTES

ACTIVITY: .... TO BE COMPLETED AT: ☐ HOME ☐ MEETING ☐ EVENT ☐ FIELD TRIP

PREP/SUPPLIES NEEDED:

WHO'S RESPONSIBLE?

(1) .... ☐ LEADER ☐ GIRL/VOLUNTEER: ....

(2) .... ☐ LEADER ☐ GIRL/VOLUNTEER: ....

(3) .... ☐ LEADER ☐ GIRL/VOLUNTEER: ....

(4) .... ☐ LEADER ☐ GIRL/VOLUNTEER: ....

(5) .... ☐ LEADER ☐ GIRL/VOLUNTEER: ....

ACTIVITY STEPS/NOTES:

LEADERSHIP KEYS: ☐ DISCOVER ☐ CONNECT ☐ TAKE ACTION   PROCESSES: ☐ GIRL-LED ☐ LEARNING BY DOING ☐ COOPERATIVE LEARNING

STEP 4:

TIME NEEDED: .... MINUTES

ACTIVITY: .... TO BE COMPLETED AT: ☐ HOME ☐ MEETING ☐ EVENT ☐ FIELD TRIP

PREP/SUPPLIES NEEDED:

WHO'S RESPONSIBLE?

(1) .... ☐ LEADER ☐ GIRL/VOLUNTEER: ....

(2) .... ☐ LEADER ☐ GIRL/VOLUNTEER: ....

(3) .... ☐ LEADER ☐ GIRL/VOLUNTEER: ....

(4) .... ☐ LEADER ☐ GIRL/VOLUNTEER: ....

(5) .... ☐ LEADER ☐ GIRL/VOLUNTEER: ....

ACTIVITY STEPS/NOTES:

LEADERSHIP KEYS: ☐ DISCOVER ☐ CONNECT ☐ TAKE ACTION   PROCESSES: ☐ GIRL-LED ☐ LEARNING BY DOING ☐ COOPERATIVE LEARNING

STEP 5:

TIME NEEDED: .... MINUTES

ACTIVITY: .... TO BE COMPLETED AT: ☐ HOME ☐ MEETING ☐ EVENT ☐ FIELD TRIP

PREP/SUPPLIES NEEDED:

WHO'S RESPONSIBLE?

(1) .... ☐ LEADER ☐ GIRL/VOLUNTEER: ....

(2) .... ☐ LEADER ☐ GIRL/VOLUNTEER: ....

(3) .... ☐ LEADER ☐ GIRL/VOLUNTEER: ....

(4) .... ☐ LEADER ☐ GIRL/VOLUNTEER: ....

(5) .... ☐ LEADER ☐ GIRL/VOLUNTEER: ....

ACTIVITY STEPS/NOTES:

LEADERSHIP KEYS: ☐ DISCOVER ☐ CONNECT ☐ TAKE ACTION   PROCESSES: ☐ GIRL-LED ☐ LEARNING BY DOING ☐ COOPERATIVE LEARNING

BADGE ACTIVITIES PLANNER

BADGE: ....

PURPOSE: ....

OF MEETINGS TO COMPLETE THIS BADGE: .... JOURNEY CONNECTION(S): .... ☐ STEP 1 ☐ STEP 2 ☐ STEP 3 ☐ STEP 4 ☐ STEP 5

LONG-TERM PLANNING:

FIELD TRIP/GUEST SPEAKER IDEAS:

STEP 1:
TIME NEEDED: .... MINUTES

ACTIVITY: .... TO BE COMPLETED AT: ☐ HOME ☐ MEETING ☐ EVENT ☐ FIELD TRIP

PREP/SUPPLIES NEEDED: WHO'S RESPONSIBLE?

(1) .... ☐ LEADER ☐ GIRL/VOLUNTEER: ....

(2) .... ☐ LEADER ☐ GIRL/VOLUNTEER: ....

(3) .... ☐ LEADER ☐ GIRL/VOLUNTEER: ....

(4) .... ☐ LEADER ☐ GIRL/VOLUNTEER: ....

(5) .... ☐ LEADER ☐ GIRL/VOLUNTEER: ....

ACTIVITY STEPS/NOTES:

LEADERSHIP KEYS: ☐ DISCOVER ☐ CONNECT ☐ TAKE ACTION   PROCESSES: ☐ GIRL-LED ☐ LEARNING BY DOING ☐ COOPERATIVE LEARNING

STEP 2:
TIME NEEDED: .... MINUTES

ACTIVITY: .... TO BE COMPLETED AT: ☐ HOME ☐ MEETING ☐ EVENT ☐ FIELD TRIP

PREP/SUPPLIES NEEDED: WHO'S RESPONSIBLE?

(1) .... ☐ LEADER ☐ GIRL/VOLUNTEER: ....

(2) .... ☐ LEADER ☐ GIRL/VOLUNTEER: ....

(3) .... ☐ LEADER ☐ GIRL/VOLUNTEER: ....

(4) .... ☐ LEADER ☐ GIRL/VOLUNTEER: ....

(5) .... ☐ LEADER ☐ GIRL/VOLUNTEER: ....

ACTIVITY STEPS/NOTES:

LEADERSHIP KEYS: ☐ DISCOVER ☐ CONNECT ☐ TAKE ACTION   PROCESSES: ☐ GIRL-LED ☐ LEARNING BY DOING ☐ COOPERATIVE LEARNING

STEP 3:

TIME NEEDED: .... MINUTES

ACTIVITY: .... TO BE COMPLETED AT: ☐ HOME ☐ MEETING ☐ EVENT ☐ FIELD TRIP

PREP/SUPPLIES NEEDED:

WHO'S RESPONSIBLE?

(1) .... ☐ LEADER ☐ GIRL/VOLUNTEER: ....

(2) .... ☐ LEADER ☐ GIRL/VOLUNTEER: ....

(3) .... ☐ LEADER ☐ GIRL/VOLUNTEER: ....

(4) .... ☐ LEADER ☐ GIRL/VOLUNTEER: ....

(5) .... ☐ LEADER ☐ GIRL/VOLUNTEER: ....

ACTIVITY STEPS/NOTES:

LEADERSHIP KEYS: ☐ DISCOVER ☐ CONNECT ☐ TAKE ACTION   PROCESSES: ☐ GIRL-LED ☐ LEARNING BY DOING ☐ COOPERATIVE LEARNING

STEP 4:

TIME NEEDED: .... MINUTES

ACTIVITY: .... TO BE COMPLETED AT: ☐ HOME ☐ MEETING ☐ EVENT ☐ FIELD TRIP

PREP/SUPPLIES NEEDED:

WHO'S RESPONSIBLE?

(1) .... ☐ LEADER ☐ GIRL/VOLUNTEER: ....

(2) .... ☐ LEADER ☐ GIRL/VOLUNTEER: ....

(3) .... ☐ LEADER ☐ GIRL/VOLUNTEER: ....

(4) .... ☐ LEADER ☐ GIRL/VOLUNTEER: ....

(5) .... ☐ LEADER ☐ GIRL/VOLUNTEER: ....

ACTIVITY STEPS/NOTES:

LEADERSHIP KEYS: ☐ DISCOVER ☐ CONNECT ☐ TAKE ACTION   PROCESSES: ☐ GIRL-LED ☐ LEARNING BY DOING ☐ COOPERATIVE LEARNING

STEP 5:

TIME NEEDED: .... MINUTES

ACTIVITY: .... TO BE COMPLETED AT: ☐ HOME ☐ MEETING ☐ EVENT ☐ FIELD TRIP

PREP/SUPPLIES NEEDED:

WHO'S RESPONSIBLE?

(1) .... ☐ LEADER ☐ GIRL/VOLUNTEER: ....

(2) .... ☐ LEADER ☐ GIRL/VOLUNTEER: ....

(3) .... ☐ LEADER ☐ GIRL/VOLUNTEER: ....

(4) .... ☐ LEADER ☐ GIRL/VOLUNTEER: ....

(5) .... ☐ LEADER ☐ GIRL/VOLUNTEER: ....

ACTIVITY STEPS/NOTES:

LEADERSHIP KEYS: ☐ DISCOVER ☐ CONNECT ☐ TAKE ACTION   PROCESSES: ☐ GIRL-LED ☐ LEARNING BY DOING ☐ COOPERATIVE LEARNING

BADGE ACTIVITIES PLANNER

BADGE:

PURPOSE: ....

OF MEETINGS TO COMPLETE THIS BADGE: .... JOURNEY CONNECTION(S): .... ☐ STEP 1 ☐ STEP 2 ☐ STEP 3 ☐ STEP 4 ☐ STEP 5

LONG-TERM PLANNING:

FIELD TRIP/GUEST SPEAKER IDEAS:

STEP 1:

TIME NEEDED: .... MINUTES

ACTIVITY: .... TO BE COMPLETED AT: ☐ HOME ☐ MEETING ☐ EVENT ☐ FIELD TRIP

PREP/SUPPLIES NEEDED:

WHO'S RESPONSIBLE?

(1) .... ☐ LEADER ☐ GIRL/VOLUNTEER: ....

(2) .... ☐ LEADER ☐ GIRL/VOLUNTEER: ....

(3) .... ☐ LEADER ☐ GIRL/VOLUNTEER: ....

(4) .... ☐ LEADER ☐ GIRL/VOLUNTEER: ....

(5) .... ☐ LEADER ☐ GIRL/VOLUNTEER: ....

ACTIVITY STEPS/NOTES:

LEADERSHIP KEYS: ☐ DISCOVER ☐ CONNECT ☐ TAKE ACTION   PROCESSES: ☐ GIRL-LED ☐ LEARNING BY DOING ☐ COOPERATIVE LEARNING

STEP 2:

TIME NEEDED: .... MINUTES

ACTIVITY: .... TO BE COMPLETED AT: ☐ HOME ☐ MEETING ☐ EVENT ☐ FIELD TRIP

PREP/SUPPLIES NEEDED:

WHO'S RESPONSIBLE?

(1) .... ☐ LEADER ☐ GIRL/VOLUNTEER: ....

(2) .... ☐ LEADER ☐ GIRL/VOLUNTEER: ....

(3) .... ☐ LEADER ☐ GIRL/VOLUNTEER: ....

(4) .... ☐ LEADER ☐ GIRL/VOLUNTEER: ....

(5) .... ☐ LEADER ☐ GIRL/VOLUNTEER: ....

ACTIVITY STEPS/NOTES:

LEADERSHIP KEYS: ☐ DISCOVER ☐ CONNECT ☐ TAKE ACTION   PROCESSES: ☐ GIRL-LED ☐ LEARNING BY DOING ☐ COOPERATIVE LEARNING

STEP 3:

TIME NEEDED: .... MINUTES

ACTIVITY: .... TO BE COMPLETED AT: ☐ HOME ☐ MEETING ☐ EVENT ☐ FIELD TRIP

PREP/SUPPLIES NEEDED:

WHO'S RESPONSIBLE?

(1) .... ☐ LEADER ☐ GIRL/VOLUNTEER: ....

(2) .... ☐ LEADER ☐ GIRL/VOLUNTEER: ....

(3) .... ☐ LEADER ☐ GIRL/VOLUNTEER: ....

(4) .... ☐ LEADER ☐ GIRL/VOLUNTEER: ....

(5) .... ☐ LEADER ☐ GIRL/VOLUNTEER: ....

ACTIVITY STEPS/NOTES:

LEADERSHIP KEYS: ☐ DISCOVER ☐ CONNECT ☐ TAKE ACTION   PROCESSES: ☐ GIRL-LED ☐ LEARNING BY DOING ☐ COOPERATIVE LEARNING

STEP 4:

TIME NEEDED: .... MINUTES

ACTIVITY: .... TO BE COMPLETED AT: ☐ HOME ☐ MEETING ☐ EVENT ☐ FIELD TRIP

PREP/SUPPLIES NEEDED:

WHO'S RESPONSIBLE?

(1) .... ☐ LEADER ☐ GIRL/VOLUNTEER: ....

(2) .... ☐ LEADER ☐ GIRL/VOLUNTEER: ....

(3) .... ☐ LEADER ☐ GIRL/VOLUNTEER: ....

(4) .... ☐ LEADER ☐ GIRL/VOLUNTEER: ....

(5) .... ☐ LEADER ☐ GIRL/VOLUNTEER: ....

ACTIVITY STEPS/NOTES:

LEADERSHIP KEYS: ☐ DISCOVER ☐ CONNECT ☐ TAKE ACTION   PROCESSES: ☐ GIRL-LED ☐ LEARNING BY DOING ☐ COOPERATIVE LEARNING

STEP 5:

TIME NEEDED: .... MINUTES

ACTIVITY: .... TO BE COMPLETED AT: ☐ HOME ☐ MEETING ☐ EVENT ☐ FIELD TRIP

PREP/SUPPLIES NEEDED:

WHO'S RESPONSIBLE?

(1) .... ☐ LEADER ☐ GIRL/VOLUNTEER: ....

(2) .... ☐ LEADER ☐ GIRL/VOLUNTEER: ....

(3) .... ☐ LEADER ☐ GIRL/VOLUNTEER: ....

(4) .... ☐ LEADER ☐ GIRL/VOLUNTEER: ....

(5) .... ☐ LEADER ☐ GIRL/VOLUNTEER: ....

ACTIVITY STEPS/NOTES:

LEADERSHIP KEYS: ☐ DISCOVER ☐ CONNECT ☐ TAKE ACTION   PROCESSES: ☐ GIRL-LED ☐ LEARNING BY DOING ☐ COOPERATIVE LEARNING

BADGE ACTIVITIES PLANNER

BADGE:

PURPOSE: ....

OF MEETINGS TO COMPLETE THIS BADGE: .... JOURNEY CONNECTION(S): .... ☐ STEP 1 ☐ STEP 2 ☐ STEP 3 ☐ STEP 4 ☐ STEP 5

LONG-TERM PLANNING:

FIELD TRIP/GUEST SPEAKER IDEAS:

STEP 1:   TIME NEEDED: .... MINUTES

ACTIVITY: .... TO BE COMPLETED AT: ☐ HOME ☐ MEETING ☐ EVENT ☐ FIELD TRIP

PREP/SUPPLIES NEEDED: WHO'S RESPONSIBLE?

(1) .... ☐ LEADER ☐ GIRL/VOLUNTEER: ....

(2) .... ☐ LEADER ☐ GIRL/VOLUNTEER: ....

(3) .... ☐ LEADER ☐ GIRL/VOLUNTEER: ....

(4) .... ☐ LEADER ☐ GIRL/VOLUNTEER: ....

(5) .... ☐ LEADER ☐ GIRL/VOLUNTEER: ....

ACTIVITY STEPS/NOTES:

LEADERSHIP KEYS: ☐ DISCOVER ☐ CONNECT ☐ TAKE ACTION   PROCESSES: ☐ GIRL-LED ☐ LEARNING BY DOING ☐ COOPERATIVE LEARNING

STEP 2:   TIME NEEDED: .... MINUTES

ACTIVITY: .... TO BE COMPLETED AT: ☐ HOME ☐ MEETING ☐ EVENT ☐ FIELD TRIP

PREP/SUPPLIES NEEDED: WHO'S RESPONSIBLE?

(1) .... ☐ LEADER ☐ GIRL/VOLUNTEER: ....

(2) .... ☐ LEADER ☐ GIRL/VOLUNTEER: ....

(3) .... ☐ LEADER ☐ GIRL/VOLUNTEER: ....

(4) .... ☐ LEADER ☐ GIRL/VOLUNTEER: ....

(5) .... ☐ LEADER ☐ GIRL/VOLUNTEER: ....

ACTIVITY STEPS/NOTES:

LEADERSHIP KEYS: ☐ DISCOVER ☐ CONNECT ☐ TAKE ACTION   PROCESSES: ☐ GIRL-LED ☐ LEARNING BY DOING ☐ COOPERATIVE LEARNING

STEP 3:

TIME NEEDED: .... MINUTES

ACTIVITY: .... TO BE COMPLETED AT: ☐ HOME ☐ MEETING ☐ EVENT ☐ FIELD TRIP

PREP/SUPPLIES NEEDED: WHO'S RESPONSIBLE?

(1) .... ☐ LEADER ☐ GIRL/VOLUNTEER: ....

(2) .... ☐ LEADER ☐ GIRL/VOLUNTEER: ....

(3) .... ☐ LEADER ☐ GIRL/VOLUNTEER: ....

(4) .... ☐ LEADER ☐ GIRL/VOLUNTEER: ....

(5) .... ☐ LEADER ☐ GIRL/VOLUNTEER: ....

ACTIVITY STEPS/NOTES:

LEADERSHIP KEYS: ☐ DISCOVER ☐ CONNECT ☐ TAKE ACTION   PROCESSES: ☐ GIRL-LED ☐ LEARNING BY DOING ☐ COOPERATIVE LEARNING

STEP 4:

TIME NEEDED: .... MINUTES

ACTIVITY: .... TO BE COMPLETED AT: ☐ HOME ☐ MEETING ☐ EVENT ☐ FIELD TRIP

PREP/SUPPLIES NEEDED: WHO'S RESPONSIBLE?

(1) .... ☐ LEADER ☐ GIRL/VOLUNTEER: ....

(2) .... ☐ LEADER ☐ GIRL/VOLUNTEER: ....

(3) .... ☐ LEADER ☐ GIRL/VOLUNTEER: ....

(4) .... ☐ LEADER ☐ GIRL/VOLUNTEER: ....

(5) .... ☐ LEADER ☐ GIRL/VOLUNTEER: ....

ACTIVITY STEPS/NOTES:

LEADERSHIP KEYS: ☐ DISCOVER ☐ CONNECT ☐ TAKE ACTION   PROCESSES: ☐ GIRL-LED ☐ LEARNING BY DOING ☐ COOPERATIVE LEARNING

STEP 5:

TIME NEEDED: .... MINUTES

ACTIVITY: .... TO BE COMPLETED AT: ☐ HOME ☐ MEETING ☐ EVENT ☐ FIELD TRIP

PREP/SUPPLIES NEEDED: WHO'S RESPONSIBLE?

(1) .... ☐ LEADER ☐ GIRL/VOLUNTEER: ....

(2) .... ☐ LEADER ☐ GIRL/VOLUNTEER: ....

(3) .... ☐ LEADER ☐ GIRL/VOLUNTEER: ....

(4) .... ☐ LEADER ☐ GIRL/VOLUNTEER: ....

(5) .... ☐ LEADER ☐ GIRL/VOLUNTEER: ....

ACTIVITY STEPS/NOTES:

LEADERSHIP KEYS: ☐ DISCOVER ☐ CONNECT ☐ TAKE ACTION   PROCESSES: ☐ GIRL-LED ☐ LEARNING BY DOING ☐ COOPERATIVE LEARNING

BADGE ACTIVITIES PLANNER

BADGE:

PURPOSE: ....

OF MEETINGS TO COMPLETE THIS BADGE: .... JOURNEY CONNECTION(S): .... ☐ STEP 1 ☐ STEP 2 ☐ STEP 3 ☐ STEP 4 ☐ STEP 5

LONG-TERM PLANNING:

FIELD TRIP/GUEST SPEAKER IDEAS:

STEP 1:   TIME NEEDED: .... MINUTES

ACTIVITY: .... TO BE COMPLETED AT: ☐ HOME ☐ MEETING ☐ EVENT ☐ FIELD TRIP

PREP/SUPPLIES NEEDED: WHO'S RESPONSIBLE?

(1) .... ☐ LEADER ☐ GIRL/VOLUNTEER: ....

(2) .... ☐ LEADER ☐ GIRL/VOLUNTEER: ....

(3) .... ☐ LEADER ☐ GIRL/VOLUNTEER: ....

(4) .... ☐ LEADER ☐ GIRL/VOLUNTEER: ....

(5) .... ☐ LEADER ☐ GIRL/VOLUNTEER: ....

ACTIVITY STEPS/NOTES:

LEADERSHIP KEYS: ☐ DISCOVER ☐ CONNECT ☐ TAKE ACTION   PROCESSES: ☐ GIRL-LED ☐ LEARNING BY DOING ☐ COOPERATIVE LEARNING

STEP 2:   TIME NEEDED: .... MINUTES

ACTIVITY: .... TO BE COMPLETED AT: ☐ HOME ☐ MEETING ☐ EVENT ☐ FIELD TRIP

PREP/SUPPLIES NEEDED: WHO'S RESPONSIBLE?

(1) .... ☐ LEADER ☐ GIRL/VOLUNTEER: ....

(2) .... ☐ LEADER ☐ GIRL/VOLUNTEER: ....

(3) .... ☐ LEADER ☐ GIRL/VOLUNTEER: ....

(4) .... ☐ LEADER ☐ GIRL/VOLUNTEER: ....

(5) .... ☐ LEADER ☐ GIRL/VOLUNTEER: ....

ACTIVITY STEPS/NOTES:

LEADERSHIP KEYS: ☐ DISCOVER ☐ CONNECT ☐ TAKE ACTION   PROCESSES: ☐ GIRL-LED ☐ LEARNING BY DOING ☐ COOPERATIVE LEARNING

STEP 3:

TIME NEEDED: .... MINUTES

ACTIVITY: .... TO BE COMPLETED AT: ☐ HOME ☐ MEETING ☐ EVENT ☐ FIELD TRIP

PREP/SUPPLIES NEEDED:

WHO'S RESPONSIBLE?

(1) .... ☐ LEADER ☐ GIRL/VOLUNTEER: ....

(2) .... ☐ LEADER ☐ GIRL/VOLUNTEER: ....

(3) .... ☐ LEADER ☐ GIRL/VOLUNTEER: ....

(4) .... ☐ LEADER ☐ GIRL/VOLUNTEER: ....

(5) .... ☐ LEADER ☐ GIRL/VOLUNTEER: ....

ACTIVITY STEPS/NOTES:

LEADERSHIP KEYS: ☐ DISCOVER ☐ CONNECT ☐ TAKE ACTION   PROCESSES: ☐ GIRL-LED ☐ LEARNING BY DOING ☐ COOPERATIVE LEARNING

STEP 4:

TIME NEEDED: .... MINUTES

ACTIVITY: .... TO BE COMPLETED AT: ☐ HOME ☐ MEETING ☐ EVENT ☐ FIELD TRIP

PREP/SUPPLIES NEEDED:

WHO'S RESPONSIBLE?

(1) .... ☐ LEADER ☐ GIRL/VOLUNTEER: ....

(2) .... ☐ LEADER ☐ GIRL/VOLUNTEER: ....

(3) .... ☐ LEADER ☐ GIRL/VOLUNTEER: ....

(4) .... ☐ LEADER ☐ GIRL/VOLUNTEER: ....

(5) .... ☐ LEADER ☐ GIRL/VOLUNTEER: ....

ACTIVITY STEPS/NOTES:

LEADERSHIP KEYS: ☐ DISCOVER ☐ CONNECT ☐ TAKE ACTION   PROCESSES: ☐ GIRL-LED ☐ LEARNING BY DOING ☐ COOPERATIVE LEARNING

STEP 5:

TIME NEEDED: .... MINUTES

ACTIVITY: .... TO BE COMPLETED AT: ☐ HOME ☐ MEETING ☐ EVENT ☐ FIELD TRIP

PREP/SUPPLIES NEEDED:

WHO'S RESPONSIBLE?

(1) .... ☐ LEADER ☐ GIRL/VOLUNTEER: ....

(2) .... ☐ LEADER ☐ GIRL/VOLUNTEER: ....

(3) .... ☐ LEADER ☐ GIRL/VOLUNTEER: ....

(4) .... ☐ LEADER ☐ GIRL/VOLUNTEER: ....

(5) .... ☐ LEADER ☐ GIRL/VOLUNTEER: ....

ACTIVITY STEPS/NOTES:

LEADERSHIP KEYS: ☐ DISCOVER ☐ CONNECT ☐ TAKE ACTION   PROCESSES: ☐ GIRL-LED ☐ LEARNING BY DOING ☐ COOPERATIVE LEARNING

BADGE ACTIVITIES PLANNER

BADGE:

PURPOSE: ....

OF MEETINGS TO COMPLETE THIS BADGE: .... JOURNEY CONNECTION(S): .... ☐ STEP 1 ☐ STEP 2 ☐ STEP 3 ☐ STEP 4 ☐ STEP 5

LONG-TERM PLANNING:

FIELD TRIP/GUEST SPEAKER IDEAS:

STEP 1:   TIME NEEDED: .... MINUTES

ACTIVITY: .... TO BE COMPLETED AT: ☐ HOME ☐ MEETING ☐ EVENT ☐ FIELD TRIP

PREP/SUPPLIES NEEDED: WHO'S RESPONSIBLE?

(1) .... ☐ LEADER ☐ GIRL/VOLUNTEER: ....

(2) .... ☐ LEADER ☐ GIRL/VOLUNTEER: ....

(3) .... ☐ LEADER ☐ GIRL/VOLUNTEER: ....

(4) .... ☐ LEADER ☐ GIRL/VOLUNTEER: ....

(5) .... ☐ LEADER ☐ GIRL/VOLUNTEER: ....

ACTIVITY STEPS/NOTES:

LEADERSHIP KEYS: ☐ DISCOVER ☐ CONNECT ☐ TAKE ACTION   PROCESSES: ☐ GIRL-LED ☐ LEARNING BY DOING ☐ COOPERATIVE LEARNING

STEP 2:   TIME NEEDED: .... MINUTES

ACTIVITY: .... TO BE COMPLETED AT: ☐ HOME ☐ MEETING ☐ EVENT ☐ FIELD TRIP

PREP/SUPPLIES NEEDED: WHO'S RESPONSIBLE?

(1) .... ☐ LEADER ☐ GIRL/VOLUNTEER: ....

(2) .... ☐ LEADER ☐ GIRL/VOLUNTEER: ....

(3) .... ☐ LEADER ☐ GIRL/VOLUNTEER: ....

(4) .... ☐ LEADER ☐ GIRL/VOLUNTEER: ....

(5) .... ☐ LEADER ☐ GIRL/VOLUNTEER: ....

ACTIVITY STEPS/NOTES:

LEADERSHIP KEYS: ☐ DISCOVER ☐ CONNECT ☐ TAKE ACTION   PROCESSES: ☐ GIRL-LED ☐ LEARNING BY DOING ☐ COOPERATIVE LEARNING

STEP 3:

TIME NEEDED: .... MINUTES

ACTIVITY: .... TO BE COMPLETED AT: ☐ HOME ☐ MEETING ☐ EVENT ☐ FIELD TRIP

PREP/SUPPLIES NEEDED:　　　　　　　　　　　　　　　　　　　　　WHO'S RESPONSIBLE?

(1) .... ☐ LEADER ☐ GIRL/VOLUNTEER: ....

(2) .... ☐ LEADER ☐ GIRL/VOLUNTEER: ....

(3) .... ☐ LEADER ☐ GIRL/VOLUNTEER: ....

(4) .... ☐ LEADER ☐ GIRL/VOLUNTEER: ....

(5) .... ☐ LEADER ☐ GIRL/VOLUNTEER: ....

ACTIVITY STEPS/NOTES:

LEADERSHIP KEYS: ☐ DISCOVER ☐ CONNECT ☐ TAKE ACTION　　　PROCESSES: ☐ GIRL-LED ☐ LEARNING BY DOING ☐ COOPERATIVE LEARNING

STEP 4:

TIME NEEDED: .... MINUTES

ACTIVITY: .... TO BE COMPLETED AT: ☐ HOME ☐ MEETING ☐ EVENT ☐ FIELD TRIP

PREP/SUPPLIES NEEDED:　　　　　　　　　　　　　　　　　　　　　WHO'S RESPONSIBLE?

(1) .... ☐ LEADER ☐ GIRL/VOLUNTEER: ....

(2) .... ☐ LEADER ☐ GIRL/VOLUNTEER: ....

(3) .... ☐ LEADER ☐ GIRL/VOLUNTEER: ....

(4) .... ☐ LEADER ☐ GIRL/VOLUNTEER: ....

(5) .... ☐ LEADER ☐ GIRL/VOLUNTEER: ....

ACTIVITY STEPS/NOTES:

LEADERSHIP KEYS: ☐ DISCOVER ☐ CONNECT ☐ TAKE ACTION　　　PROCESSES: ☐ GIRL-LED ☐ LEARNING BY DOING ☐ COOPERATIVE LEARNING

STEP 5:

TIME NEEDED: .... MINUTES

ACTIVITY: .... TO BE COMPLETED AT: ☐ HOME ☐ MEETING ☐ EVENT ☐ FIELD TRIP

PREP/SUPPLIES NEEDED:　　　　　　　　　　　　　　　　　　　　　WHO'S RESPONSIBLE?

(1) .... ☐ LEADER ☐ GIRL/VOLUNTEER: ....

(2) .... ☐ LEADER ☐ GIRL/VOLUNTEER: ....

(3) .... ☐ LEADER ☐ GIRL/VOLUNTEER: ....

(4) .... ☐ LEADER ☐ GIRL/VOLUNTEER: ....

(5) .... ☐ LEADER ☐ GIRL/VOLUNTEER: ....

ACTIVITY STEPS/NOTES:

LEADERSHIP KEYS: ☐ DISCOVER ☐ CONNECT ☐ TAKE ACTION　　　PROCESSES: ☐ GIRL-LED ☐ LEARNING BY DOING ☐ COOPERATIVE LEARNING

BADGE ACTIVITIES PLANNER

BADGE: ....

PURPOSE: ....

OF MEETINGS TO COMPLETE THIS BADGE: .... JOURNEY CONNECTION(S): .... ☐ STEP 1 ☐ STEP 2 ☐ STEP 3 ☐ STEP 4 ☐ STEP 5

LONG-TERM PLANNING:

FIELD TRIP/GUEST SPEAKER IDEAS:

STEP 1:   TIME NEEDED: .... MINUTES

ACTIVITY: .... TO BE COMPLETED AT: ☐ HOME ☐ MEETING ☐ EVENT ☐ FIELD TRIP

PREP/SUPPLIES NEEDED: WHO'S RESPONSIBLE?

(1) .... ☐ LEADER ☐ GIRL/VOLUNTEER: ....

(2) .... ☐ LEADER ☐ GIRL/VOLUNTEER: ....

(3) .... ☐ LEADER ☐ GIRL/VOLUNTEER: ....

(4) .... ☐ LEADER ☐ GIRL/VOLUNTEER: ....

(5) .... ☐ LEADER ☐ GIRL/VOLUNTEER: ....

ACTIVITY STEPS/NOTES:

LEADERSHIP KEYS: ☐ DISCOVER ☐ CONNECT ☐ TAKE ACTION   PROCESSES: ☐ GIRL-LED ☐ LEARNING BY DOING ☐ COOPERATIVE LEARNING

STEP 2:   TIME NEEDED: .... MINUTES

ACTIVITY: .... TO BE COMPLETED AT: ☐ HOME ☐ MEETING ☐ EVENT ☐ FIELD TRIP

PREP/SUPPLIES NEEDED: WHO'S RESPONSIBLE?

(1) .... ☐ LEADER ☐ GIRL/VOLUNTEER: ....

(2) .... ☐ LEADER ☐ GIRL/VOLUNTEER: ....

(3) .... ☐ LEADER ☐ GIRL/VOLUNTEER: ....

(4) .... ☐ LEADER ☐ GIRL/VOLUNTEER: ....

(5) .... ☐ LEADER ☐ GIRL/VOLUNTEER: ....

ACTIVITY STEPS/NOTES:

LEADERSHIP KEYS: ☐ DISCOVER ☐ CONNECT ☐ TAKE ACTION   PROCESSES: ☐ GIRL-LED ☐ LEARNING BY DOING ☐ COOPERATIVE LEARNING

STEP 3:

TIME NEEDED: .... MINUTES

ACTIVITY: ....   TO BE COMPLETED AT: ☐ HOME ☐ MEETING ☐ EVENT ☐ FIELD TRIP

PREP/SUPPLIES NEEDED:

WHO'S RESPONSIBLE?

(1) ....   ☐ LEADER ☐ GIRL/VOLUNTEER: ....

(2) ....   ☐ LEADER ☐ GIRL/VOLUNTEER: ....

(3) ....   ☐ LEADER ☐ GIRL/VOLUNTEER: ....

(4) ....   ☐ LEADER ☐ GIRL/VOLUNTEER: ....

(5) ....   ☐ LEADER ☐ GIRL/VOLUNTEER: ....

ACTIVITY STEPS/NOTES:

LEADERSHIP KEYS: ☐ DISCOVER ☐ CONNECT ☐ TAKE ACTION   PROCESSES: ☐ GIRL-LED ☐ LEARNING BY DOING ☐ COOPERATIVE LEARNING

STEP 4:

TIME NEEDED: .... MINUTES

ACTIVITY: ....   TO BE COMPLETED AT: ☐ HOME ☐ MEETING ☐ EVENT ☐ FIELD TRIP

PREP/SUPPLIES NEEDED:

WHO'S RESPONSIBLE?

(1) ....   ☐ LEADER ☐ GIRL/VOLUNTEER: ....

(2) ....   ☐ LEADER ☐ GIRL/VOLUNTEER: ....

(3) ....   ☐ LEADER ☐ GIRL/VOLUNTEER: ....

(4) ....   ☐ LEADER ☐ GIRL/VOLUNTEER: ....

(5) ....   ☐ LEADER ☐ GIRL/VOLUNTEER: ....

ACTIVITY STEPS/NOTES:

LEADERSHIP KEYS: ☐ DISCOVER ☐ CONNECT ☐ TAKE ACTION   PROCESSES: ☐ GIRL-LED ☐ LEARNING BY DOING ☐ COOPERATIVE LEARNING

STEP 5:

TIME NEEDED: .... MINUTES

ACTIVITY: ....   TO BE COMPLETED AT: ☐ HOME ☐ MEETING ☐ EVENT ☐ FIELD TRIP

PREP/SUPPLIES NEEDED:

WHO'S RESPONSIBLE?

(1) ....   ☐ LEADER ☐ GIRL/VOLUNTEER: ....

(2) ....   ☐ LEADER ☐ GIRL/VOLUNTEER: ....

(3) ....   ☐ LEADER ☐ GIRL/VOLUNTEER: ....

(4) ....   ☐ LEADER ☐ GIRL/VOLUNTEER: ....

(5) ....   ☐ LEADER ☐ GIRL/VOLUNTEER: ....

ACTIVITY STEPS/NOTES:

LEADERSHIP KEYS: ☐ DISCOVER ☐ CONNECT ☐ TAKE ACTION   PROCESSES: ☐ GIRL-LED ☐ LEARNING BY DOING ☐ COOPERATIVE LEARNING

BADGE ACTIVITIES PLANNER

BADGE:

PURPOSE: ....

OF MEETINGS TO COMPLETE THIS BADGE: .... JOURNEY CONNECTION(S): .... ☐ STEP 1 ☐ STEP 2 ☐ STEP 3 ☐ STEP 4 ☐ STEP 5

LONG-TERM PLANNING:

FIELD TRIP/GUEST SPEAKER IDEAS:

STEP 1:   TIME NEEDED: .... MINUTES

ACTIVITY: .... TO BE COMPLETED AT: ☐ HOME ☐ MEETING ☐ EVENT ☐ FIELD TRIP

PREP/SUPPLIES NEEDED: WHO'S RESPONSIBLE?

(1) .... ☐ LEADER ☐ GIRL/VOLUNTEER: ....

(2) .... ☐ LEADER ☐ GIRL/VOLUNTEER: ....

(3) .... ☐ LEADER ☐ GIRL/VOLUNTEER: ....

(4) .... ☐ LEADER ☐ GIRL/VOLUNTEER: ....

(5) .... ☐ LEADER ☐ GIRL/VOLUNTEER: ....

ACTIVITY STEPS/NOTES:

LEADERSHIP KEYS: ☐ DISCOVER ☐ CONNECT ☐ TAKE ACTION   PROCESSES: ☐ GIRL-LED ☐ LEARNING BY DOING ☐ COOPERATIVE LEARNING

STEP 2:   TIME NEEDED: .... MINUTES

ACTIVITY: .... TO BE COMPLETED AT: ☐ HOME ☐ MEETING ☐ EVENT ☐ FIELD TRIP

PREP/SUPPLIES NEEDED: WHO'S RESPONSIBLE?

(1) .... ☐ LEADER ☐ GIRL/VOLUNTEER: ....

(2) .... ☐ LEADER ☐ GIRL/VOLUNTEER: ....

(3) .... ☐ LEADER ☐ GIRL/VOLUNTEER: ....

(4) .... ☐ LEADER ☐ GIRL/VOLUNTEER: ....

(5) .... ☐ LEADER ☐ GIRL/VOLUNTEER: ....

ACTIVITY STEPS/NOTES:

LEADERSHIP KEYS: ☐ DISCOVER ☐ CONNECT ☐ TAKE ACTION   PROCESSES: ☐ GIRL-LED ☐ LEARNING BY DOING ☐ COOPERATIVE LEARNING

STEP 3:

TIME NEEDED: .... MINUTES

ACTIVITY: .... TO BE COMPLETED AT: ☐ HOME ☐ MEETING ☐ EVENT ☐ FIELD TRIP

PREP/SUPPLIES NEEDED:

WHO'S RESPONSIBLE?

(1) .... ☐ LEADER ☐ GIRL/VOLUNTEER: ....

(2) .... ☐ LEADER ☐ GIRL/VOLUNTEER: ....

(3) .... ☐ LEADER ☐ GIRL/VOLUNTEER: ....

(4) .... ☐ LEADER ☐ GIRL/VOLUNTEER: ....

(5) .... ☐ LEADER ☐ GIRL/VOLUNTEER: ....

ACTIVITY STEPS/NOTES:

LEADERSHIP KEYS: ☐ DISCOVER ☐ CONNECT ☐ TAKE ACTION   PROCESSES: ☐ GIRL-LED ☐ LEARNING BY DOING ☐ COOPERATIVE LEARNING

STEP 4:

TIME NEEDED: .... MINUTES

ACTIVITY: .... TO BE COMPLETED AT: ☐ HOME ☐ MEETING ☐ EVENT ☐ FIELD TRIP

PREP/SUPPLIES NEEDED:

WHO'S RESPONSIBLE?

(1) .... ☐ LEADER ☐ GIRL/VOLUNTEER: ....

(2) .... ☐ LEADER ☐ GIRL/VOLUNTEER: ....

(3) .... ☐ LEADER ☐ GIRL/VOLUNTEER: ....

(4) .... ☐ LEADER ☐ GIRL/VOLUNTEER: ....

(5) .... ☐ LEADER ☐ GIRL/VOLUNTEER: ....

ACTIVITY STEPS/NOTES:

LEADERSHIP KEYS: ☐ DISCOVER ☐ CONNECT ☐ TAKE ACTION   PROCESSES: ☐ GIRL-LED ☐ LEARNING BY DOING ☐ COOPERATIVE LEARNING

STEP 5:

TIME NEEDED: .... MINUTES

ACTIVITY: .... TO BE COMPLETED AT: ☐ HOME ☐ MEETING ☐ EVENT ☐ FIELD TRIP

PREP/SUPPLIES NEEDED:

WHO'S RESPONSIBLE?

(1) .... ☐ LEADER ☐ GIRL/VOLUNTEER: ....

(2) .... ☐ LEADER ☐ GIRL/VOLUNTEER: ....

(3) .... ☐ LEADER ☐ GIRL/VOLUNTEER: ....

(4) .... ☐ LEADER ☐ GIRL/VOLUNTEER: ....

(5) .... ☐ LEADER ☐ GIRL/VOLUNTEER: ....

ACTIVITY STEPS/NOTES:

LEADERSHIP KEYS: ☐ DISCOVER ☐ CONNECT ☐ TAKE ACTION   PROCESSES: ☐ GIRL-LED ☐ LEARNING BY DOING ☐ COOPERATIVE LEARNING

BADGE ACTIVITIES PLANNER

BADGE:

PURPOSE: ....

OF MEETINGS TO COMPLETE THIS BADGE: .... JOURNEY CONNECTION(S): .... ☐ STEP 1 ☐ STEP 2 ☐ STEP 3 ☐ STEP 4 ☐ STEP 5

LONG-TERM PLANNING:

FIELD TRIP/GUEST SPEAKER IDEAS:

STEP 1:   TIME NEEDED: .... MINUTES

ACTIVITY: .... TO BE COMPLETED AT: ☐ HOME ☐ MEETING ☐ EVENT ☐ FIELD TRIP

PREP/SUPPLIES NEEDED: WHO'S RESPONSIBLE?

(1) .... ☐ LEADER ☐ GIRL/VOLUNTEER: ....

(2) .... ☐ LEADER ☐ GIRL/VOLUNTEER: ....

(3) .... ☐ LEADER ☐ GIRL/VOLUNTEER: ....

(4) .... ☐ LEADER ☐ GIRL/VOLUNTEER: ....

(5) .... ☐ LEADER ☐ GIRL/VOLUNTEER: ....

ACTIVITY STEPS/NOTES:

LEADERSHIP KEYS: ☐ DISCOVER ☐ CONNECT ☐ TAKE ACTION   PROCESSES: ☐ GIRL-LED ☐ LEARNING BY DOING ☐ COOPERATIVE LEARNING

STEP 2:   TIME NEEDED: .... MINUTES

ACTIVITY: .... TO BE COMPLETED AT: ☐ HOME ☐ MEETING ☐ EVENT ☐ FIELD TRIP

PREP/SUPPLIES NEEDED: WHO'S RESPONSIBLE?

(1) .... ☐ LEADER ☐ GIRL/VOLUNTEER: ....

(2) .... ☐ LEADER ☐ GIRL/VOLUNTEER: ....

(3) .... ☐ LEADER ☐ GIRL/VOLUNTEER: ....

(4) .... ☐ LEADER ☐ GIRL/VOLUNTEER: ....

(5) .... ☐ LEADER ☐ GIRL/VOLUNTEER: ....

ACTIVITY STEPS/NOTES:

LEADERSHIP KEYS: ☐ DISCOVER ☐ CONNECT ☐ TAKE ACTION   PROCESSES: ☐ GIRL-LED ☐ LEARNING BY DOING ☐ COOPERATIVE LEARNING

STEP 3:

TIME NEEDED: .... MINUTES

ACTIVITY: .... TO BE COMPLETED AT: ☐ HOME ☐ MEETING ☐ EVENT ☐ FIELD TRIP

PREP/SUPPLIES NEEDED:

WHO'S RESPONSIBLE?

(1) .... ☐ LEADER ☐ GIRL/VOLUNTEER: ....

(2) .... ☐ LEADER ☐ GIRL/VOLUNTEER: ....

(3) .... ☐ LEADER ☐ GIRL/VOLUNTEER: ....

(4) .... ☐ LEADER ☐ GIRL/VOLUNTEER: ....

(5) .... ☐ LEADER ☐ GIRL/VOLUNTEER: ....

ACTIVITY STEPS/NOTES:

LEADERSHIP KEYS: ☐ DISCOVER ☐ CONNECT ☐ TAKE ACTION   PROCESSES: ☐ GIRL-LED ☐ LEARNING BY DOING ☐ COOPERATIVE LEARNING

STEP 4:

TIME NEEDED: .... MINUTES

ACTIVITY: .... TO BE COMPLETED AT: ☐ HOME ☐ MEETING ☐ EVENT ☐ FIELD TRIP

PREP/SUPPLIES NEEDED:

WHO'S RESPONSIBLE?

(1) .... ☐ LEADER ☐ GIRL/VOLUNTEER: ....

(2) .... ☐ LEADER ☐ GIRL/VOLUNTEER: ....

(3) .... ☐ LEADER ☐ GIRL/VOLUNTEER: ....

(4) .... ☐ LEADER ☐ GIRL/VOLUNTEER: ....

(5) .... ☐ LEADER ☐ GIRL/VOLUNTEER: ....

ACTIVITY STEPS/NOTES:

LEADERSHIP KEYS: ☐ DISCOVER ☐ CONNECT ☐ TAKE ACTION   PROCESSES: ☐ GIRL-LED ☐ LEARNING BY DOING ☐ COOPERATIVE LEARNING

STEP 5:

TIME NEEDED: .... MINUTES

ACTIVITY: .... TO BE COMPLETED AT: ☐ HOME ☐ MEETING ☐ EVENT ☐ FIELD TRIP

PREP/SUPPLIES NEEDED:

WHO'S RESPONSIBLE?

(1) .... ☐ LEADER ☐ GIRL/VOLUNTEER: ....

(2) .... ☐ LEADER ☐ GIRL/VOLUNTEER: ....

(3) .... ☐ LEADER ☐ GIRL/VOLUNTEER: ....

(4) .... ☐ LEADER ☐ GIRL/VOLUNTEER: ....

(5) .... ☐ LEADER ☐ GIRL/VOLUNTEER: ....

ACTIVITY STEPS/NOTES:

LEADERSHIP KEYS: ☐ DISCOVER ☐ CONNECT ☐ TAKE ACTION   PROCESSES: ☐ GIRL-LED ☐ LEARNING BY DOING ☐ COOPERATIVE LEARNING

BADGE ACTIVITIES PLANNER

BADGE: ....

PURPOSE: ....

OF MEETINGS TO COMPLETE THIS BADGE: .... JOURNEY CONNECTION(S): .... ☐ STEP 1 ☐ STEP 2 ☐ STEP 3 ☐ STEP 4 ☐ STEP 5

LONG-TERM PLANNING:

FIELD TRIP/GUEST SPEAKER IDEAS:

STEP 1:   TIME NEEDED: .... MINUTES

ACTIVITY: .... TO BE COMPLETED AT: ☐ HOME ☐ MEETING ☐ EVENT ☐ FIELD TRIP

PREP/SUPPLIES NEEDED: WHO'S RESPONSIBLE?

(1) ....   ☐ LEADER ☐ GIRL/VOLUNTEER: ....

(2) ....   ☐ LEADER ☐ GIRL/VOLUNTEER: ....

(3) ....   ☐ LEADER ☐ GIRL/VOLUNTEER: ....

(4) ....   ☐ LEADER ☐ GIRL/VOLUNTEER: ....

(5) ....   ☐ LEADER ☐ GIRL/VOLUNTEER: ....

ACTIVITY STEPS/NOTES:

LEADERSHIP KEYS: ☐ DISCOVER ☐ CONNECT ☐ TAKE ACTION   PROCESSES: ☐ GIRL-LED ☐ LEARNING BY DOING ☐ COOPERATIVE LEARNING

STEP 2:   TIME NEEDED: .... MINUTES

ACTIVITY: .... TO BE COMPLETED AT: ☐ HOME ☐ MEETING ☐ EVENT ☐ FIELD TRIP

PREP/SUPPLIES NEEDED: WHO'S RESPONSIBLE?

(1) ....   ☐ LEADER ☐ GIRL/VOLUNTEER: ....

(2) ....   ☐ LEADER ☐ GIRL/VOLUNTEER: ....

(3) ....   ☐ LEADER ☐ GIRL/VOLUNTEER: ....

(4) ....   ☐ LEADER ☐ GIRL/VOLUNTEER: ....

(5) ....   ☐ LEADER ☐ GIRL/VOLUNTEER: ....

ACTIVITY STEPS/NOTES:

LEADERSHIP KEYS: ☐ DISCOVER ☐ CONNECT ☐ TAKE ACTION   PROCESSES: ☐ GIRL-LED ☐ LEARNING BY DOING ☐ COOPERATIVE LEARNING

STEP 3:

TIME NEEDED: .... MINUTES

ACTIVITY: .... TO BE COMPLETED AT: ☐ HOME ☐ MEETING ☐ EVENT ☐ FIELD TRIP

PREP/SUPPLIES NEEDED: WHO'S RESPONSIBLE?

(1) .... ☐ LEADER ☐ GIRL/VOLUNTEER: ....

(2) .... ☐ LEADER ☐ GIRL/VOLUNTEER: ....

(3) .... ☐ LEADER ☐ GIRL/VOLUNTEER: ....

(4) .... ☐ LEADER ☐ GIRL/VOLUNTEER: ....

(5) .... ☐ LEADER ☐ GIRL/VOLUNTEER: ....

ACTIVITY STEPS/NOTES:

LEADERSHIP KEYS: ☐ DISCOVER ☐ CONNECT ☐ TAKE ACTION   PROCESSES: ☐ GIRL-LED ☐ LEARNING BY DOING ☐ COOPERATIVE LEARNING

STEP 4:

TIME NEEDED: .... MINUTES

ACTIVITY: .... TO BE COMPLETED AT: ☐ HOME ☐ MEETING ☐ EVENT ☐ FIELD TRIP

PREP/SUPPLIES NEEDED: WHO'S RESPONSIBLE?

(1) .... ☐ LEADER ☐ GIRL/VOLUNTEER: ....

(2) .... ☐ LEADER ☐ GIRL/VOLUNTEER: ....

(3) .... ☐ LEADER ☐ GIRL/VOLUNTEER: ....

(4) .... ☐ LEADER ☐ GIRL/VOLUNTEER: ....

(5) .... ☐ LEADER ☐ GIRL/VOLUNTEER: ....

ACTIVITY STEPS/NOTES:

LEADERSHIP KEYS: ☐ DISCOVER ☐ CONNECT ☐ TAKE ACTION   PROCESSES: ☐ GIRL-LED ☐ LEARNING BY DOING ☐ COOPERATIVE LEARNING

STEP 5:

TIME NEEDED: .... MINUTES

ACTIVITY: .... TO BE COMPLETED AT: ☐ HOME ☐ MEETING ☐ EVENT ☐ FIELD TRIP

PREP/SUPPLIES NEEDED: WHO'S RESPONSIBLE?

(1) .... ☐ LEADER ☐ GIRL/VOLUNTEER: ....

(2) .... ☐ LEADER ☐ GIRL/VOLUNTEER: ....

(3) .... ☐ LEADER ☐ GIRL/VOLUNTEER: ....

(4) .... ☐ LEADER ☐ GIRL/VOLUNTEER: ....

(5) .... ☐ LEADER ☐ GIRL/VOLUNTEER: ....

ACTIVITY STEPS/NOTES:

LEADERSHIP KEYS: ☐ DISCOVER ☐ CONNECT ☐ TAKE ACTION   PROCESSES: ☐ GIRL-LED ☐ LEARNING BY DOING ☐ COOPERATIVE LEARNING

TRACKER:

CUSTOMIZE THIS TRACKER TO MEET YOUR NEEDS! RECORD ATTENDANCE, DUES, BADGES, ETC.

TROOPS WITH 5-10 MEMBERS: LIST YOUR MEETINGS/DUES/PAPERWORK/BADGES/PRODUCTS IN THE FIRST COLUMN AND YOUR GIRL'S NAMES IN THE ANGLED COLUMN HEADERS.

TROOPS WITH 10+ MEMBERS: LIST YOUR GIRL'S NAMES IN THE FIRST COLUMN AND YOUR MEETINGS/DUES/PAPERWORK/BADGES/PRODUCTS IN THE ANGLED COLUMN HEADERS.

TRACKER:

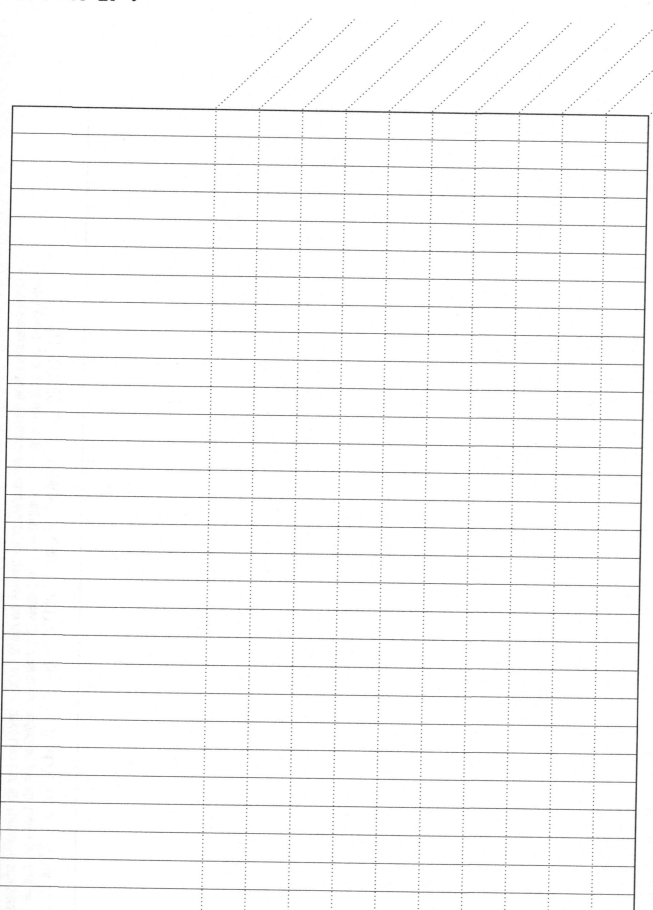

CUSTOMIZE THIS TRACKER TO MEET YOUR NEEDS! RECORD ATTENDANCE, DUES, BADGES, ETC.

TROOPS WITH 5-10 MEMBERS: LIST YOUR MEETINGS/DUES/PAPERWORK/BADGES/PRODUCTS IN THE FIRST COLUMN AND YOUR GIRL'S NAMES IN THE ANGLED COLUMN HEADERS.

TROOPS WITH 10+ MEMBERS: LIST YOUR GIRL'S NAMES IN THE FIRST COLUMN AND YOUR MEETINGS/DUES/PAPERWORK/BADGES/PRODUCTS IN THE ANGLED COLUMN HEADERS.

TRACKER:

CUSTOMIZE THIS TRACKER TO MEET YOUR NEEDS! RECORD ATTENDANCE, DUES, BADGES, ETC.

TROOPS WITH 5-10 MEMBERS: LIST YOUR MEETINGS/DUES/PAPERWORK/BADGES/PRODUCTS IN THE FIRST COLUMN AND YOUR GIRL'S NAMES IN THE ANGLED COLUMN HEADERS.

TROOPS WITH 10+ MEMBERS: LIST YOUR GIRL'S NAMES IN THE FIRST COLUMN AND YOUR MEETINGS/DUES/PAPERWORK/BADGES/PRODUCTS IN THE ANGLED COLUMN HEADERS.

TRACKER:

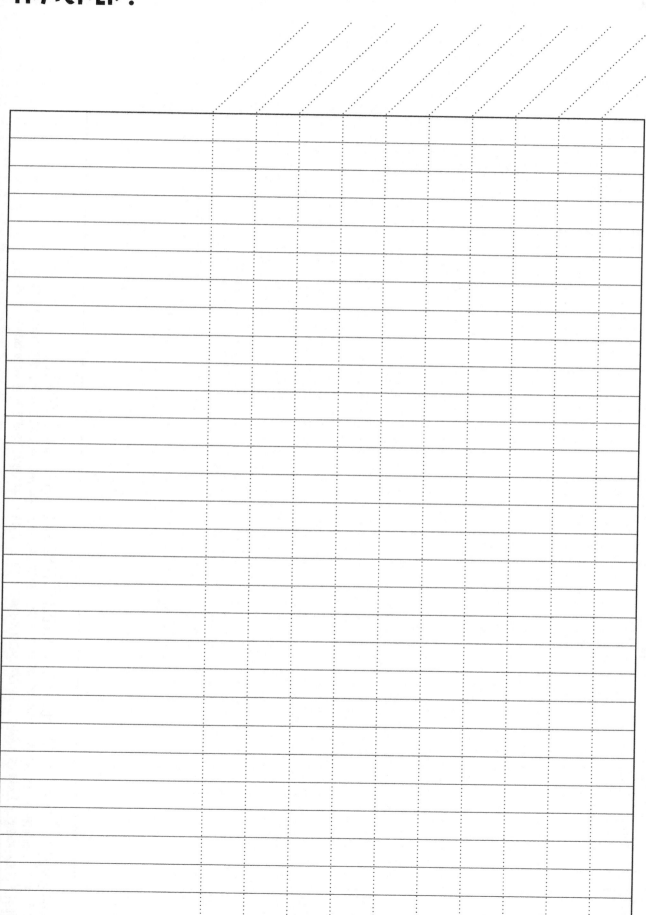

CUSTOMIZE THIS TRACKER TO MEET YOUR NEEDS! RECORD ATTENDANCE, DUES, BADGES, ETC.

TROOPS WITH 5-10 MEMBERS: LIST YOUR MEETINGS/DUES/PAPERWORK/BADGES/PRODUCTS IN THE FIRST COLUMN AND YOUR GIRL'S NAMES IN THE ANGLED COLUMN HEADERS.

TROOPS WITH 10+ MEMBERS: LIST YOUR GIRL'S NAMES IN THE FIRST COLUMN AND YOUR MEETINGS/DUES/PAPERWORK/BADGES/PRODUCTS IN THE ANGLED COLUMN HEADERS.

TRACKER:

CUSTOMIZE THIS TRACKER TO MEET YOUR NEEDS! RECORD ATTENDANCE, DUES, BADGES, ETC.

TROOPS WITH 5-10 MEMBERS: LIST YOUR MEETINGS/DUES/PAPERWORK/BADGES/PRODUCTS IN THE FIRST COLUMN AND YOUR GIRL'S NAMES IN THE ANGLED COLUMN HEADERS.

TROOPS WITH 10+ MEMBERS: LIST YOUR GIRL'S NAMES IN THE FIRST COLUMN AND YOUR MEETINGS/DUES/PAPERWORK/BADGES/PRODUCTS IN THE ANGLED COLUMN HEADERS.

TRACKER:

CUSTOMIZE THIS TRACKER TO MEET YOUR NEEDS! RECORD ATTENDANCE, DUES, BADGES, ETC.
TROOPS WITH 5-10 MEMBERS: LIST YOUR MEETINGS/DUES/PAPERWORK/BADGES/PRODUCTS IN THE FIRST COLUMN AND YOUR GIRL'S NAMES IN THE ANGLED COLUMN HEADERS.
TROOPS WITH 10+ MEMBERS: LIST YOUR GIRL'S NAMES IN THE FIRST COLUMN AND YOUR MEETINGS/DUES/PAPERWORK/BADGES/PRODUCTS IN THE ANGLED COLUMN HEADERS.

TRACKER:

CUSTOMIZE THIS TRACKER TO MEET YOUR NEEDS: RECORD ATTENDANCE, DUES, BADGES, ETC.

TROOPS WITH 5-10 MEMBERS: LIST YOUR MEETINGS/DUES/PAPERWORK/BADGES/PRODUCTS IN THE FIRST COLUMN AND YOUR GIRL'S NAMES IN THE ANGLED COLUMN HEADERS.

TROOPS WITH 10+ MEMBERS: LIST YOUR GIRL'S NAMES IN THE FIRST COLUMN AND YOUR MEETINGS/DUES/PAPERWORK/BADGES/PRODUCTS IN THE ANGLED COLUMN HEADERS.

TRACKER:

CUSTOMIZE THIS TRACKER TO MEET YOUR NEEDS! RECORD ATTENDANCE, DUES, BADGES, ETC.

TROOPS WITH 5-10 MEMBERS: LIST YOUR MEETINGS/DUES/PAPERWORK/BADGES/PRODUCTS IN THE FIRST COLUMN AND YOUR GIRL'S NAMES IN THE ANGLED COLUMN HEADERS.

TROOPS WITH 10+ MEMBERS: LIST YOUR GIRL'S NAMES IN THE FIRST COLUMN AND YOUR MEETINGS/DUES/PAPERWORK/BADGES/PRODUCTS IN THE ANGLED COLUMN HEADERS.

TRACKER:

CUSTOMIZE THIS TRACKER TO MEET YOUR NEEDS! RECORD ATTENDANCE, DUES, BADGES, ETC.
TROOPS WITH 5-10 MEMBERS: LIST YOUR MEETINGS/DUES/PAPERWORK/BADGES/PRODUCTS IN THE FIRST COLUMN AND YOUR GIRL'S NAMES IN THE ANGLED COLUMN HEADERS.
TROOPS WITH 10+ MEMBERS: LIST YOUR GIRL'S NAMES IN THE FIRST COLUMN AND YOUR MEETINGS/DUES/PAPERWORK/BADGES/PRODUCTS IN THE ANGLED COLUMN HEADERS.

TRACKER:

CUSTOMIZE THIS TRACKER TO MEET YOUR NEEDS! RECORD ATTENDANCE, DUES, BADGES, ETC.

TROOPS WITH 5-10 MEMBERS: LIST YOUR MEETINGS/DUES/PAPERWORK/BADGES/PRODUCTS IN THE FIRST COLUMN AND YOUR GIRL'S NAMES IN THE ANGLED COLUMN HEADERS.

TROOPS WITH 10+ MEMBERS: LIST YOUR GIRL'S NAMES IN THE FIRST COLUMN AND YOUR MEETINGS/DUES/PAPERWORK/BADGES/PRODUCTS IN THE ANGLED COLUMN HEADERS.

TROOP DUES & BUDGET PLANNER

OF GIRLS: .... # OF VOLUNTEERS: .... # OF MEETINGS: .... NOTES:

TROOP EXPENSES   TOTAL TROOP EXPENSES: $ ....

PROGRAMS, EVENTS & FIELD TRIPS

(1)	$.......... X .... = $..........	(11)	$.......... X .... = $..........
(2)	$.......... X .... = $..........	(12)	$.......... X .... = $..........
(3)	$.......... X .... = $..........	(13)	$.......... X .... = $..........
(4)	$.......... X .... = $..........	(14)	$.......... X .... = $..........
(5)	$.......... X .... = $..........	(15)	$.......... X .... = $..........
(6)	$.......... X .... = $..........	(16)	$.......... X .... = $..........
(7)	$.......... X .... = $..........	(17)	$.......... X .... = $..........
(8)	$.......... X .... = $..........	(18)	$.......... X .... = $..........
(9)	$.......... X .... = $..........	(19)	$.......... X .... = $..........
(10)	$.......... X .... = $..........	(20)	$.......... X .... = $..........

TOTAL FOR PROGRAMS, EVENTS & FIELD TRIPS: $

UNIFORMS, BADGES & INSIGNIA

UNIFORMS	$.......... X .... = $..........	FUN PATCHES	$.......... X .... = $..........
GIRL SCOUTING GUIDES	$.......... X .... = $..........	OTHER:	$.......... X .... = $..........
JOURNEYS	$.......... X .... = $..........	OTHER:	$.......... X .... = $..........
BADGES	$.......... X .... = $..........	OTHER:	$.......... X .... = $..........

TOTAL FOR UNIFORMS, BADGES & INSIGNIA: $

SUPPLIES, SNACKS & OTHER EXPENSES

ANNUAL MEMBERSHIP FEES	$.......... X .... = $..........	COOKIE BOOTH SETUP	$.......... X .... = $..........
SERVICE UNIT DUES	$.......... X .... = $..........	CEREMONIES/CELEBRATIONS	$.......... X .... = $..........
ANNUAL FUND DONATIONS	$.......... X .... = $..........	CHARITABLE CONTRIBUTIONS	$.......... X .... = $..........
TROOP NECESSITIES	$.......... X .... = $..........	OTHER:	$.......... X .... = $..........
BADGE ACTIVITY SUPPLIES	$.......... X .... = $..........	OTHER:	$.......... X .... = $..........
SNACKS	$.......... X .... = $..........	OTHER:	$.......... X .... = $..........

TOTAL FOR SUPPLIES, SNACKS & OTHER EXPENSES: $

PARENT/GUARDIAN CONTRIBUTIONS

TOTAL PARENT/GUARDIAN CONTRIBUTIONS: $ ....

PROGRAMS, EVENTS & FIELD TRIPS: $ ....

FUN PATCHES: $ ....

BADGE ACTIVITY SUPPLIES: $ ....

UNIFORMS: $ ....

ANNUAL MEMBERSHIP FEES: $ ....

SNACKS: $ ....

GIRL SCOUTING GUIDES: $ ....

SERVICE UNIT DUES: $ ....

COOKIE BOOTH SETUP: $ ....

JOURNEYS: $ ....

ANNUAL FUND DONATIONS: $ ....

OTHER: ....

BADGES: $ ....

TROOP NECESSITIES: $ ....

OTHER: ....

TOTAL TROOP EXPENSES ($ ....) MINUS TOTAL CONTRIBUTIONS FROM PARENTS/GUARDIANS ($ ....) = REMAINING TROOP EXPENSES ($ ....)

TROOP INCOME

TOTAL ESTIMATED TROOP INCOME: $ ....

FALL PRODUCT SALES

☐ TROOP WILL PARTICIPATE ☐ TROOP WILL NOT PARTICIPATE

TROOP PROFIT PER SALE: .... # OF GIRLS PARTICIPATING: .... SALES REQUIRED TO COVER REMAINING TROOP EXPENSES: $ .... ☐ ACHIEVABLE ☐ UNREALISTIC

TOTAL ESTIMATED FALL PRODUCT PROFIT: $ .... GROSS SALES OUR TROOP MUST MAKE TO ACHIEVE THIS ESTIMATED PROFIT: $ ....

COOKIE SALES

☐ TROOP WILL PARTICIPATE ☐ TROOP WILL NOT PARTICIPATE

TROOP PROFIT PER BOX: $ .... # OF GIRLS PARTICIPATING: .... SALES REQUIRED TO COVER REMAINING TROOP EXPENSES: .... ☐ ACHIEVEABLE ☐ UNREALISTIC

TOTAL ESTIMATED COOKIE PROFIT: $ .... # OF BOXES OUR TROOP MUST SELL TO ACHIEVE THIS ESTIMATED PROFIT: ....

OTHER COUNCIL-APPROVED MONEY-EARNING ACTIVITIES

☐ TROOP WILL PARTICIPATE ☐ TROOP WILL NOT PARTICIPATE

(1) .... : $ .... (2) .... : $ .... (3) .... : $ ....

TOTAL ESTIMATED PROFIT FROM OTHER COUNCIL-APPROVED MONEY-EARNING ACTIVITIES: $ ....

TROOP DUES

STARTING ACCOUNT BALANCE: $ .... ☐ 100% IS RESERVED FOR A TRIP, ETC. ☐ 100% CAN BE USED TO COVER EXPENSES ☐ $ .... CAN BE USED TO COVER EXPENSES

TROOP DUES CALCULATOR:

$ .... + $ .... + $ .... = $ .... - $ .... = $ ....

| AVAILABLE FUNDS FROM ACCOUNT BALANCE | PARENT/GUARDIAN CONTRIBUTIONS | TOTAL ESTIMATED TROOP INCOME | | TOTAL TROOP EXPENSES | TOTAL TROOP DUES |

TOTAL TROOP DUES ($ ....) DIVIDED BY THE NUMBER OF GIRLS (..........) = TROOP DUES PER GIRL ($ ....)

TROOP DUES WILL BE COLLECTED ☐ UPFRONT ☐ AT EACH MEETING (TROOP DUES PER GIRL DIVIDED BY # OF MEETINGS = $ ....)

NOTES:

TROOP FINANCES

<table>
<tr><td colspan="2">CHECKING ACCOUNT DETAILS</td><td>STARTING BALANCE AS OF ...... / ...... / ...... : $ ....</td></tr>
</table>

BANK: .... LOCATION: .... HOURS: ....

ACCOUNT NUMBER: .... ROUTING NUMBER: .... DEBIT CARD NUMBER: .... CVV: ....

NOTES:

DATE	CHECK/DEBIT	DESCRIPTION	WITHDRAWAL	DEPOSIT	BALANCE
	☐ CHECK # ☐ DEBIT CARD				
	☐ CHECK # ☐ DEBIT CARD				
	☐ CHECK # ☐ DEBIT CARD				
	☐ CHECK # ☐ DEBIT CARD				
	☐ CHECK # ☐ DEBIT CARD				
	☐ CHECK # ☐ DEBIT CARD				
	☐ CHECK # ☐ DEBIT CARD				
	☐ CHECK # ☐ DEBIT CARD				
	☐ CHECK # ☐ DEBIT CARD				
	☐ CHECK # ☐ DEBIT CARD				
	☐ CHECK # ☐ DEBIT CARD				
	☐ CHECK # ☐ DEBIT CARD				
	☐ CHECK # ☐ DEBIT CARD				
	☐ CHECK # ☐ DEBIT CARD				
	☐ CHECK # ☐ DEBIT CARD				
	☐ CHECK # ☐ DEBIT CARD				
	☐ CHECK # ☐ DEBIT CARD				
	☐ CHECK # ☐ DEBIT CARD				
	☐ CHECK # ☐ DEBIT CARD				
	☐ CHECK # ☐ DEBIT CARD				
	☐ CHECK # ☐ DEBIT CARD				

"IF PEOPLE ARE GOING TO JUDGE ME WITHOUT FULLY UNDERSTANDING THE CONTENT OF MY CHARACTER, THEN THEIR OPINION JUST ISN'T WORTH IT."

LGBTQ+ RIGHTS ACTIVIST JAZZ JENNINGS

DATE	CHECK/DEBIT	DESCRIPTION	WITHDRAWAL	DEPOSIT	BALANCE
	☐ CHECK # ☐ DEBIT CARD				
	☐ CHECK # ☐ DEBIT CARD				
	☐ CHECK # ☐ DEBIT CARD				
	☐ CHECK # ☐ DEBIT CARD				
	☐ CHECK # ☐ DEBIT CARD				
	☐ CHECK # ☐ DEBIT CARD				
	☐ CHECK # ☐ DEBIT CARD				
	☐ CHECK # ☐ DEBIT CARD				
	☐ CHECK # ☐ DEBIT CARD				
	☐ CHECK # ☐ DEBIT CARD				
	☐ CHECK # ☐ DEBIT CARD				
	☐ CHECK # ☐ DEBIT CARD				
	☐ CHECK # ☐ DEBIT CARD				
	☐ CHECK # ☐ DEBIT CARD				
	☐ CHECK # ☐ DEBIT CARD				
	☐ CHECK # ☐ DEBIT CARD				
	☐ CHECK # ☐ DEBIT CARD				
	☐ CHECK # ☐ DEBIT CARD				
	☐ CHECK # ☐ DEBIT CARD				
	☐ CHECK # ☐ DEBIT CARD				
	☐ CHECK # ☐ DEBIT CARD				
	☐ CHECK # ☐ DEBIT CARD				
	☐ CHECK # ☐ DEBIT CARD				

TROOP LEADER TAX-DEDUCTIBLE EXPENSES

DATE	EXPENSE	COST	DATE	EXPENSE	COST

TROOP LEADER TAX-DEDUCTIBLE MILEAGE

DATE	PURPOSE	MILES	DATE	PURPOSE	MILES

COOKIE BOOTH PLANNER

TROOP COOKIE MANAGER(S): ....

COOKIE BOOTH NOTES:

DATE & TIME	COOKIE BOOTH LOCATION	VOLUNTEERS		GIRLS
		(1)	(1)	(3)
		(2)	(2)	(4)
M T W TH F SAT SUN				
		(1)	(1)	(3)
		(2)	(2)	(4)
M T W TH F SAT SUN				
		(1)	(1)	(3)
		(2)	(2)	(4)
M T W TH F SAT SUN				
		(1)	(1)	(3)
		(2)	(2)	(4)
M T W TH F SAT SUN				
		(1)	(1)	(3)
		(2)	(2)	(4)
M T W TH F SAT SUN				
		(1)	(1)	(3)
		(2)	(2)	(4)
M T W TH F SAT SUN				
		(1)	(1)	(3)
		(2)	(2)	(4)
M T W TH F SAT SUN				
		(1)	(1)	(3)
		(2)	(2)	(4)
M T W TH F SAT SUN				

COOKIE BOOTH NOTES:

DATE & TIME	COOKIE BOOTH LOCATION	VOLUNTEERS		GIRLS	
M T W TH F SAT SUN		(1) (2)	(1) (2)	(3) (4)	
M T W TH F SAT SUN		(1) (2)	(1) (2)	(3) (4)	
M T W TH F SAT SUN		(1) (2)	(1) (2)	(3) (4)	
M T W TH F SAT SUN		(1) (2)	(1) (2)	(3) (4)	
M T W TH F SAT SUN		(1) (2)	(1) (2)	(3) (4)	
M T W TH F SAT SUN		(1) (2)	(1) (2)	(3) (4)	
M T W TH F SAT SUN		(1) (2)	(1) (2)	(3) (4)	
M T W TH F SAT SUN		(1) (2)	(1) (2)	(3) (4)	

COOKIE BOOTH SALES TRACKER

COOKIE BOOTH LOCATION: _____   TOTAL CASH & CREDIT CARD SALES: $ _____

DATE: ...../...../.....   STARTING TIME: ....   ENDING TIME: ....   VOLUNTEERS: ....

	PRICE PER BOX	STARTING # OF BOXES	ENDING # OF BOXES	BOXES SOLD	CASH SALES	CREDIT CARD SALES
THIN MINTS	$				$	$
SAMOAS / CARAMEL DELITES	$				$	$
TAGALONGS / PEANUT BUTTER PATTIES	$				$	$
TREFOILS / SHORTBREAD	$				$	$
DO-SI-DOS / PEANUT BUTTER SANDWICH	$				$	$
SAVANNAH SMILES	$				$	$
TOFFEE-TASTIC	$				$	$
THANKS-A-LOT	$				$	$
S'MORES	$				$	$
LEMONADES	$				$	$
CARAMEL CHOCOLATE CHIP	$				$	$
TOTALS:		....	....	....	$	$ ....
		STARTING # OF BOXES	ENDING # OF BOXES	BOXES SOLD	CASH SALES	CREDIT CARD SALES

STARTING # OF BOXES (..........) MINUS ENDING # OF BOXES (..........) = TOTAL BOXES SOLD (..........) ☐ SAME AS ABOVE (YAY!) ☐ DIFFERENT FROM ABOVE (UH-OH)

ENDING CASH ($..........) MINUS STARTING CASH ($..........) = TOTAL CASH SALES ($..........) ☐ SAME AS ABOVE (YAY!) ☐ DIFFERENT FROM ABOVE (UH-OH)

COOKIE BOOTH HOURS

GIRL	START TIME	END TIME	TOTAL HOURS	BOXES SOLD	GIRL	START TIME	END TIME	TOTAL HOURS	BOXES SOLD

NOTES:

TOTAL ESTIMATED TROOP PROFIT FROM THIS COOKIE BOOTH: $ _____

COOKIE BOOTH LOCATION:

TOTAL CASH & CREDIT CARD SALES: $ ....

DATE: ...../...../.....   STARTING TIME: ....   ENDING TIME: ....   VOLUNTEERS: ....

	PRICE PER BOX	STARTING # OF BOXES	ENDING # OF BOXES	BOXES SOLD	CASH SALES	CREDIT CARD SALES
THIN MINTS	$				$	$
SAMOAS / CARAMEL DELITES	$				$	$
TAGALONGS / PEANUT BUTTER PATTIES	$				$	$
TREFOILS / SHORTBREAD	$				$	$
DO-SI-DOS / PEANUT BUTTER SANDWICH	$				$	$
SAVANNAH SMILES	$				$	$
TOFFEE-TASTIC	$				$	$
THANKS-A-LOT	$				$	$
S'MORES	$				$	$
LEMONADES	$				$	$
CARAMEL CHOCOLATE CHIP	$				$	$
TOTALS:		.... STARTING # OF BOXES	.... ENDING # OF BOXES	.... BOXES SOLD	$.............. CASH SALES	$.............. CREDIT CARD SALES

STARTING # OF BOXES (.........) MINUS ENDING # OF BOXES (.........) = TOTAL BOXES SOLD (.........) ☐ SAME AS ABOVE (YAY!) ☐ DIFFERENT FROM ABOVE (UH-OH)

ENDING CASH ($.........) MINUS STARTING CASH ($.........) = TOTAL CASH SALES ($.........) ☐ SAME AS ABOVE (YAY!) ☐ DIFFERENT FROM ABOVE (UH-OH)

COOKIE BOOTH HOURS

GIRL	START TIME	END TIME	TOTAL HOURS	BOXES SOLD	GIRL	START TIME	END TIME	TOTAL HOURS	BOXES SOLD

TES:

TOTAL ESTIMATED TROOP PROFIT FROM THIS COOKIE BOOTH: $ ....

COOKIE BOOTH SALES TRACKER

COOKIE BOOTH LOCATION: _____   TOTAL CASH & CREDIT CARD SALES: $ _____

DATE: ___/___/___   **STARTING TIME:** _____   **ENDING TIME:** _____   **VOLUNTEERS:** _____

	PRICE PER BOX	STARTING # OF BOXES	ENDING # OF BOXES	BOXES SOLD	CASH SALES	CREDIT CARD SALES
THIN MINTS	$				$	$
SAMOAS / CARAMEL DELITES	$				$	$
TAGALONGS / PEANUT BUTTER PATTIES	$				$	$
TREFOILS / SHORTBREAD	$				$	$
DO-SI-DOS / PEANUT BUTTER SANDWICH	$				$	$
SAVANNAH SMILES	$				$	$
TOFFEE-TASTIC	$				$	$
THANKS-A-LOT	$				$	$
S'MORES	$				$	$
LEMONADES	$				$	$
CARAMEL CHOCOLATE CHIP	$				$	$
TOTALS:		_____	_____	_____	$ _____	$ _____
		STARTING # OF BOXES	ENDING # OF BOXES	BOXES SOLD	CASH SALES	CREDIT CARD SALES

STARTING # OF BOXES (_____) MINUS ENDING # OF BOXES (_____) = TOTAL BOXES SOLD (_____) ☐ SAME AS ABOVE (YAY!) ☐ DIFFERENT FROM ABOVE (UH-OH)

ENDING CASH ($ _____) MINUS STARTING CASH ($ _____) = TOTAL CASH SALES ($ _____) ☐ SAME AS ABOVE (YAY!) ☐ DIFFERENT FROM ABOVE (UH-OH)

COOKIE BOOTH HOURS

GIRL	START TIME	END TIME	TOTAL HOURS	BOXES SOLD	GIRL	START TIME	END TIME	TOTAL HOURS	BOXES SOLD

NOTES:

TOTAL ESTIMATED TROOP PROFIT FROM THIS COOKIE BOOTH: $ _____

COOKIE BOOTH LOCATION:

TOTAL CASH & CREDIT CARD SALES: $ ....

DATE: ...../...../.....   STARTING TIME: ....   ENDING TIME: ....   VOLUNTEERS: ....

	PRICE PER BOX	STARTING # OF BOXES	ENDING # OF BOXES	BOXES SOLD	CASH SALES	CREDIT CARD SALES
THIN MINTS	$				$	$
SAMOAS / CARAMEL DELITES	$				$	$
TAGALONGS / PEANUT BUTTER PATTIES	$				$	$
TREFOILS / SHORTBREAD	$				$	$
DO-SI-DOS / PEANUT BUTTER SANDWICH	$				$	$
SAVANNAH SMILES	$				$	$
TOFFEE-TASTIC	$				$	$
THANKS-A-LOT	$				$	$
S'MORES	$				$	$
LEMONADES	$				$	$
CARAMEL CHOCOLATE CHIP	$				$	$
TOTALS:		STARTING # OF BOXES	ENDING # OF BOXES	BOXES SOLD	$ CASH SALES	$ CREDIT CARD SALES

STARTING # OF BOXES (..........) MINUS ENDING # OF BOXES (..........) = TOTAL BOXES SOLD (..........) ☐ SAME AS ABOVE (YAY!) ☐ DIFFERENT FROM ABOVE (UH-OH)

ENDING CASH ($..........) MINUS STARTING CASH ($..........) = TOTAL CASH SALES ($..........) ☐ SAME AS ABOVE (YAY!) ☐ DIFFERENT FROM ABOVE (UH-OH)

COOKIE BOOTH HOURS

GIRL	START TIME	END TIME	TOTAL HOURS	BOXES SOLD	GIRL	START TIME	END TIME	TOTAL HOURS	BOXES SOLD

S:

TOTAL ESTIMATED TROOP PROFIT FROM THIS COOKIE BOOTH: $ ....

COOKIE BOOTH SALES TRACKER

COOKIE BOOTH LOCATION: _____   TOTAL CASH & CREDIT CARD SALES: $ _____

DATE: ___/___/___   STARTING TIME: _____   ENDING TIME: _____   VOLUNTEERS: _____

	PRICE PER BOX	STARTING # OF BOXES	ENDING # OF BOXES	BOXES SOLD	CASH SALES	CREDIT CARD SALES
THIN MINTS	$				$	$
SAMOAS / CARAMEL DELITES	$				$	$
TAGALONGS / PEANUT BUTTER PATTIES	$				$	$
TREFOILS / SHORTBREAD	$				$	$
DO-SI-DOS / PEANUT BUTTER SANDWICH	$				$	$
SAVANNAH SMILES	$				$	$
TOFFEE-TASTIC	$				$	$
THANKS-A-LOT	$				$	$
S'MORES	$				$	$
LEMONADES	$				$	$
CARAMEL CHOCOLATE CHIP	$				$	$
TOTALS:		....	....	....	$	$ ....
		STARTING # OF BOXES	ENDING # OF BOXES	BOXES SOLD	CASH SALES	CREDIT CARD SALES

STARTING # OF BOXES (..........) MINUS ENDING # OF BOXES (..........) = TOTAL BOXES SOLD (..........) ☐ SAME AS ABOVE (YAY!) ☐ DIFFERENT FROM ABOVE (UH-OH)

ENDING CASH ($ ....) MINUS STARTING CASH ($ ....) = TOTAL CASH SALES ($ ....) ☐ SAME AS ABOVE (YAY!) ☐ DIFFERENT FROM ABOVE (UH-OH)

COOKIE BOOTH HOURS

GIRL	START TIME	END TIME	TOTAL HOURS	BOXES SOLD	GIRL	START TIME	END TIME	TOTAL HOURS	BOXES SOLD

NOTES:

TOTAL ESTIMATED TROOP PROFIT FROM THIS COOKIE BOOTH: $ _____

"GIVING MYSELF GRACE IN MOMENTS OF DOUBT HAS HELPED ME GAIN CONFIDENCE IN WHATEVER I'M DOING, EVEN OUTSIDE OF GYMNASTICS."

OLYMPIC GOLD MEDALIST SUNI LEE

COOKIE BOOTH LOCATION:

TOTAL CASH & CREDIT CARD SALES: $ ....

DATE: ...../...../...... STARTING TIME: .... ENDING TIME: .... VOLUNTEERS: ....

	PRICE PER BOX	STARTING # OF BOXES	ENDING # OF BOXES	BOXES SOLD	CASH SALES	CREDIT CARD SALES
THIN MINTS	$				$	$
SAMOAS / CARAMEL DELITES	$				$	$
TAGALONGS / PEANUT BUTTER PATTIES	$				$	$
TREFOILS / SHORTBREAD	$				$	$
DO-SI-DOS / PEANUT BUTTER SANDWICH	$				$	$
SAVANNAH SMILES	$				$	$
TOFFEE-TASTIC	$				$	$
THANKS-A-LOT	$				$	$
S'MORES	$				$	$
LEMONADES	$				$	$
CARAMEL CHOCOLATE CHIP	$				$	$
TOTALS:		....	....	....	$..............	$..............
		STARTING # OF BOXES	ENDING # OF BOXES	BOXES SOLD	CASH SALES	CREDIT CARD SALES

STARTING # OF BOXES (..........) MINUS ENDING # OF BOXES (..........) = TOTAL BOXES SOLD (..........) ☐ SAME AS ABOVE (YAY!) ☐ DIFFERENT FROM ABOVE (UH-OH)

ENDING CASH ($..........) MINUS STARTING CASH ($..........) = TOTAL CASH SALES ($..........) ☐ SAME AS ABOVE (YAY!) ☐ DIFFERENT FROM ABOVE (UH-OH)

COOKIE BOOTH HOURS

GIRL	START TIME	END TIME	TOTAL HOURS	BOXES SOLD	GIRL	START TIME	END TIME	TOTAL HOURS	BOXES SOLD

ES:

TOTAL ESTIMATED TROOP PROFIT FROM THIS COOKIE BOOTH: $ ....

COOKIE BOOTH SALES TRACKER

COOKIE BOOTH LOCATION: _____   TOTAL CASH & CREDIT CARD SALES: $ _____

DATE: ___ / ___ / ___   STARTING TIME: _____   ENDING TIME: _____   VOLUNTEERS: _____

	PRICE PER BOX	STARTING # OF BOXES	ENDING # OF BOXES	BOXES SOLD	CASH SALES	CREDIT CARD SALES
THIN MINTS	$				$	$
SAMOAS / CARAMEL DELITES	$				$	$
TAGALONGS / PEANUT BUTTER PATTIES	$				$	$
TREFOILS / SHORTBREAD	$				$	$
DO-SI-DOS / PEANUT BUTTER SANDWICH	$				$	$
SAVANNAH SMILES	$				$	$
TOFFEE-TASTIC	$				$	$
THANKS-A-LOT	$				$	$
S'MORES	$				$	$
LEMONADES	$				$	$
CARAMEL CHOCOLATE CHIP	$				$	$
TOTALS:		....	....	....	$	$ ....
		STARTING # OF BOXES	ENDING # OF BOXES	BOXES SOLD	CASH SALES	CREDIT CARD SALES

STARTING # OF BOXES (..........) MINUS ENDING # OF BOXES (..........) = TOTAL BOXES SOLD (..........) ☐ SAME AS ABOVE (YAY!) ☐ DIFFERENT FROM ABOVE (UH-OH)

ENDING CASH ($..........) MINUS STARTING CASH ($..........) = TOTAL CASH SALES ($..........) ☐ SAME AS ABOVE (YAY!) ☐ DIFFERENT FROM ABOVE (UH-OH)

COOKIE BOOTH HOURS

GIRL	START TIME	END TIME	TOTAL HOURS	BOXES SOLD	GIRL	START TIME	END TIME	TOTAL HOURS	BOXES SOLD

NOTES:

TOTAL ESTIMATED TROOP PROFIT FROM THIS COOKIE BOOTH: $ _____

"MOST ACTIONS YOU TAKE WON'T IMPACT EVERYONE, BUT IT IS THE IMPRESSIONS YOU LEAVE ON A FEW PEOPLE AT A TIME THAT WILL ADD UP TO SOMETHING BIG."

WOMEN'S RIGHTS ADVOCATE PAXTON SMITH

COOKIE BOOTH LOCATION:

TOTAL CASH & CREDIT CARD SALES: $ ....

DATE: ..... / ..... / ..... STARTING TIME: .... ENDING TIME: .... VOLUNTEERS: ....

	PRICE PER BOX	STARTING # OF BOXES	ENDING # OF BOXES	BOXES SOLD	CASH SALES	CREDIT CARD SALES
THIN MINTS	$				$	$
SAMOAS / CARAMEL DELITES	$				$	$
TAGALONGS / PEANUT BUTTER PATTIES	$				$	$
TREFOILS / SHORTBREAD	$				$	$
DO-SI-DOS / PEANUT BUTTER SANDWICH	$				$	$
SAVANNAH SMILES	$				$	$
TOFFEE-TASTIC	$				$	$
THANKS-A-LOT	$				$	$
S'MORES	$				$	$
LEMONADES	$				$	$
CARAMEL CHOCOLATE CHIP	$				$	$
TOTALS:					$	$
	STARTING # OF BOXES	ENDING # OF BOXES	BOXES SOLD		CASH SALES	CREDIT CARD SALES

STARTING # OF BOXES (.........) MINUS ENDING # OF BOXES (.........) = TOTAL BOXES SOLD (.........) ☐ SAME AS ABOVE (YAY!) ☐ DIFFERENT FROM ABOVE (UH-OH)

ENDING CASH ($ ....) MINUS STARTING CASH ($ ....) = TOTAL CASH SALES ($ ....) ☐ SAME AS ABOVE (YAY!) ☐ DIFFERENT FROM ABOVE (UH-OH)

COOKIE BOOTH HOURS

GIRL	START TIME	END TIME	TOTAL HOURS	BOXES SOLD	GIRL	START TIME	END TIME	TOTAL HOURS	BOXES SOLD

ES:

TOTAL ESTIMATED TROOP PROFIT FROM THIS COOKIE BOOTH: $ ....

COOKIE BOOTH SALES TRACKER

COOKIE BOOTH LOCATION: _____

TOTAL CASH & CREDIT CARD SALES: $ _____

DATE: ...../...../.....   STARTING TIME: ....   ENDING TIME: ....   VOLUNTEERS: ....

	PRICE PER BOX	STARTING # OF BOXES	ENDING # OF BOXES	BOXES SOLD	CASH SALES	CREDIT CARD SALES
THIN MINTS	$				$	$
SAMOAS / CARAMEL DELITES	$				$	$
TAGALONGS / PEANUT BUTTER PATTIES	$				$	$
TREFOILS / SHORTBREAD	$				$	$
DO-SI-DOS / PEANUT BUTTER SANDWICH	$				$	$
SAVANNAH SMILES	$				$	$
TOFFEE-TASTIC	$				$	$
THANKS-A-LOT	$				$	$
S'MORES	$				$	$
LEMONADES	$				$	$
CARAMEL CHOCOLATE CHIP	$				$	$
TOTALS:		....	....	....	$...............	$...............
		STARTING # OF BOXES	ENDING # OF BOXES	BOXES SOLD	CASH SALES	CREDIT CARD SALES

STARTING # OF BOXES (............) MINUS ENDING # OF BOXES (............) = TOTAL BOXES SOLD (............) ☐ SAME AS ABOVE (YAY!) ☐ DIFFERENT FROM ABOVE (UH-OH)

ENDING CASH ($............) MINUS STARTING CASH ($............) = TOTAL CASH SALES ($............) ☐ SAME AS ABOVE (YAY!) ☐ DIFFERENT FROM ABOVE (UH-OH)

COOKIE BOOTH HOURS

GIRL	START TIME	END TIME	TOTAL HOURS	BOXES SOLD	GIRL	START TIME	END TIME	TOTAL HOURS	BOXES SOLD

NOTES:

TOTAL ESTIMATED TROOP PROFIT FROM THIS COOKIE BOOTH: $ ....

COOKIE BOOTH LOCATION:

TOTAL CASH & CREDIT CARD SALES: $ ....

DATE: ..../..../.... STARTING TIME: .... ENDING TIME: .... VOLUNTEERS: ....

	PRICE PER BOX	STARTING # OF BOXES	ENDING # OF BOXES	BOXES SOLD	CASH SALES	CREDIT CARD SALES
THIN MINTS	$				$	$
SAMOAS / CARAMEL DELITES	$				$	$
TAGALONGS / PEANUT BUTTER PATTIES	$				$	$
TREFOILS / SHORTBREAD	$				$	$
DO-SI-DOS / PEANUT BUTTER SANDWICH	$				$	$
SAVANNAH SMILES	$				$	$
TOFFEE-TASTIC	$				$	$
THANKS-A-LOT	$				$	$
S'MORES	$				$	$
LEMONADES	$				$	$
CARAMEL CHOCOLATE CHIP	$				$	$
TOTALS:		.... STARTING # OF BOXES	.... ENDING # OF BOXES	.... BOXES SOLD	$.......... CASH SALES	$.......... CREDIT CARD SALES

STARTING # OF BOXES (..........) MINUS ENDING # OF BOXES (..........) = TOTAL BOXES SOLD (..........) ☐ SAME AS ABOVE (YAY!) ☐ DIFFERENT FROM ABOVE (UH-OH)

ENDING CASH ($..........) MINUS STARTING CASH ($..........) = TOTAL CASH SALES ($..........) ☐ SAME AS ABOVE (YAY!) ☐ DIFFERENT FROM ABOVE (UH-OH)

COOKIE BOOTH HOURS

GIRL	START TIME	END TIME	TOTAL HOURS	BOXES SOLD	GIRL	START TIME	END TIME	TOTAL HOURS	BOXES SOLD

ES:

TOTAL ESTIMATED TROOP PROFIT FROM THIS COOKIE BOOTH: $ ....

VOLUNTEER SIGN-UP

NOTES FOR VOLUNTEERS:

DATE & TIME	MEETING / EVENT	# OF VOLUNTEERS NEEDED	VOLUNTEER NAMES & PHONE NUMBERS
M T W TH F SAT SUN	☐ MEETING ☐ COOKIE BOOTH ☐ EVENT:		
M T W TH F SAT SUN	☐ MEETING ☐ COOKIE BOOTH ☐ EVENT:		
M T W TH F SAT SUN	☐ MEETING ☐ COOKIE BOOTH ☐ EVENT:		
M T W TH F SAT SUN	☐ MEETING ☐ COOKIE BOOTH ☐ EVENT:		
M T W TH F SAT SUN	☐ MEETING ☐ COOKIE BOOTH ☐ EVENT:		
M T W TH F SAT SUN	☐ MEETING ☐ COOKIE BOOTH ☐ EVENT:		
M T W TH F SAT SUN	☐ MEETING ☐ COOKIE BOOTH ☐ EVENT:		
M T W TH F SAT SUN	☐ MEETING ☐ COOKIE BOOTH ☐ EVENT:		

NOTES FOR VOLUNTEERS:

DATE & TIME	MEETING / EVENT	# OF VOLUNTEERS NEEDED	VOLUNTEER NAMES & PHONE NUMBERS
M T W TH F SAT SUN	☐ MEETING ☐ COOKIE BOOTH ☐ EVENT:		
M T W TH F SAT SUN	☐ MEETING ☐ COOKIE BOOTH ☐ EVENT:		
M T W TH F SAT SUN	☐ MEETING ☐ COOKIE BOOTH ☐ EVENT:		
M T W TH F SAT SUN	☐ MEETING ☐ COOKIE BOOTH ☐ EVENT:		
M T W TH F SAT SUN	☐ MEETING ☐ COOKIE BOOTH ☐ EVENT:		
M T W TH F SAT SUN	☐ MEETING ☐ COOKIE BOOTH ☐ EVENT:		
M T W TH F SAT SUN	☐ MEETING ☐ COOKIE BOOTH ☐ EVENT:		
M T W TH F SAT SUN	☐ MEETING ☐ COOKIE BOOTH ☐ EVENT:		

VOLUNTEER SIGN-UP

NOTES FOR VOLUNTEERS:

DATE & TIME	MEETING / EVENT	# OF VOLUNTEERS NEEDED	VOLUNTEER NAMES & PHONE NUMBERS
M T W TH F SAT SUN	☐ MEETING ☐ COOKIE BOOTH ☐ EVENT:		
M T W TH F SAT SUN	☐ MEETING ☐ COOKIE BOOTH ☐ EVENT:		
M T W TH F SAT SUN	☐ MEETING ☐ COOKIE BOOTH ☐ EVENT:		
M T W TH F SAT SUN	☐ MEETING ☐ COOKIE BOOTH ☐ EVENT:		
M T W TH F SAT SUN	☐ MEETING ☐ COOKIE BOOTH ☐ EVENT:		
M T W TH F SAT SUN	☐ MEETING ☐ COOKIE BOOTH ☐ EVENT:		
M T W TH F SAT SUN	☐ MEETING ☐ COOKIE BOOTH ☐ EVENT:		
M T W TH F SAT SUN	☐ MEETING ☐ COOKIE BOOTH ☐ EVENT:		

NOTES FOR VOLUNTEERS:

DATE & TIME	MEETING / EVENT	# OF VOLUNTEERS NEEDED	VOLUNTEER NAMES & PHONE NUMBERS
M T W TH F SAT SUN	☐ MEETING ☐ COOKIE BOOTH ☐ EVENT:		
M T W TH F SAT SUN	☐ MEETING ☐ COOKIE BOOTH ☐ EVENT:		
M T W TH F SAT SUN	☐ MEETING ☐ COOKIE BOOTH ☐ EVENT:		
M T W TH F SAT SUN	☐ MEETING ☐ COOKIE BOOTH ☐ EVENT:		
M T W TH F SAT SUN	☐ MEETING ☐ COOKIE BOOTH ☐ EVENT:		
M T W TH F SAT SUN	☐ MEETING ☐ COOKIE BOOTH ☐ EVENT:		
M T W TH F SAT SUN	☐ MEETING ☐ COOKIE BOOTH ☐ EVENT:		
M T W TH F SAT SUN	☐ MEETING ☐ COOKIE BOOTH ☐ EVENT:		

VOLUNTEER SIGN-UP

NOTES FOR VOLUNTEERS:

DATE & TIME	MEETING / EVENT	# OF VOLUNTEERS NEEDED	VOLUNTEER NAMES & PHONE NUMBERS
M T W TH F SAT SUN	☐ MEETING ☐ COOKIE BOOTH ☐ EVENT:		
M T W TH F SAT SUN	☐ MEETING ☐ COOKIE BOOTH ☐ EVENT:		
M T W TH F SAT SUN	☐ MEETING ☐ COOKIE BOOTH ☐ EVENT:		
M T W TH F SAT SUN	☐ MEETING ☐ COOKIE BOOTH ☐ EVENT:		
M T W TH F SAT SUN	☐ MEETING ☐ COOKIE BOOTH ☐ EVENT:		
M T W TH F SAT SUN	☐ MEETING ☐ COOKIE BOOTH ☐ EVENT:		
M T W TH F SAT SUN	☐ MEETING ☐ COOKIE BOOTH ☐ EVENT:		
M T W TH F SAT SUN	☐ MEETING ☐ COOKIE BOOTH ☐ EVENT:		

NOTES FOR VOLUNTEERS:

DATE & TIME	MEETING / EVENT	# OF VOLUNTEERS NEEDED	VOLUNTEER NAMES & PHONE NUMBERS
M T W TH F SAT SUN	☐ MEETING ☐ COOKIE BOOTH ☐ EVENT:		
M T W TH F SAT SUN	☐ MEETING ☐ COOKIE BOOTH ☐ EVENT:		
M T W TH F SAT SUN	☐ MEETING ☐ COOKIE BOOTH ☐ EVENT:		
M T W TH F SAT SUN	☐ MEETING ☐ COOKIE BOOTH ☐ EVENT:		
M T W TH F SAT SUN	☐ MEETING ☐ COOKIE BOOTH ☐ EVENT:		
M T W TH F SAT SUN	☐ MEETING ☐ COOKIE BOOTH ☐ EVENT:		
M T W TH F SAT SUN	☐ MEETING ☐ COOKIE BOOTH ☐ EVENT:		
M T W TH F SAT SUN	☐ MEETING ☐ COOKIE BOOTH ☐ EVENT:		

SNACK SIGN-UP

SNACK SUGGESTIONS:

INGREDIENTS TO AVOID:

PLEASE BRING SNACKS FOR .... PEOPLE.

DATE	MEETING / EVENT	VOLUNTEER NAME & PHONE NUMBER
	☐ MEETING ☐ EVENT:	
	☐ MEETING ☐ EVENT:	
	☐ MEETING ☐ EVENT:	
	☐ MEETING ☐ EVENT:	
	☐ MEETING ☐ EVENT:	
	☐ MEETING ☐ EVENT:	
	☐ MEETING ☐ EVENT:	
	☐ MEETING ☐ EVENT:	
	☐ MEETING ☐ EVENT:	
	☐ MEETING ☐ EVENT:	
	☐ MEETING ☐ EVENT:	
	☐ MEETING ☐ EVENT:	
	☐ MEETING ☐ EVENT:	

SNACK SUGGESTIONS:

INGREDIENTS TO AVOID:

PLEASE BRING SNACKS FOR .... PEOPLE.

DATE	MEETING / EVENT	VOLUNTEER NAME & PHONE NUMBER
	☐ MEETING ☐ EVENT:	
	☐ MEETING ☐ EVENT:	
	☐ MEETING ☐ EVENT:	
	☐ MEETING ☐ EVENT:	
	☐ MEETING ☐ EVENT:	
	☐ MEETING ☐ EVENT:	
	☐ MEETING ☐ EVENT:	
	☐ MEETING ☐ EVENT:	
	☐ MEETING ☐ EVENT:	
	☐ MEETING ☐ EVENT:	
	☐ MEETING ☐ EVENT:	
	☐ MEETING ☐ EVENT:	
	☐ MEETING ☐ EVENT:	

VOLUNTEER DRIVER LOG

NAME: ☐ BACKGROUND CHECK

PHONE: (......) .... DRIVER'S LICENSE #: .... EXPIRATION: ...... / ...... / ...... LICENSE PLATE: ....

VEHICLE YEAR, MAKE & MODEL: .... # OF PASSENGER SEATBELTS: ....

CAR INSURANCE COMPANY: .... POLICY #: .... EXPIRATION: ...... / ...... / ......

DRIVING LOG:

DATE	EVENT/DESTINATION	DRIVER SIGNATURE	TROOP LEADER SIGNATURE

NAME: ☐ BACKGROUND CHECK

PHONE: (......) .... DRIVER'S LICENSE #: .... EXPIRATION: ...... / ...... / ...... LICENSE PLATE: ....

VEHICLE YEAR, MAKE & MODEL: .... # OF PASSENGER SEATBELTS: ....

CAR INSURANCE COMPANY: .... POLICY #: .... EXPIRATION: ...... / ...... / ......

DRIVING LOG:

DATE	EVENT/DESTINATION	DRIVER SIGNATURE	TROOP LEADER SIGNATURE

"NO MATTER WHAT'S KEEPING YOU FROM BEING YOUR AUTHENTIC SELF, HOLD ONTO THE HOPE THAT THERE WILL BE AN END TO THAT ROAD. THERE WILL BE."
ACTRESS & LGBTQ+ RIGHTS ACTIVIST JOSIE TOTAH

NAME:

☐ BACKGROUND CHECK

PHONE: (......) .... DRIVER'S LICENSE #: .... EXPIRATION: ...../...../..... LICENSE PLATE: ....

VEHICLE YEAR, MAKE & MODEL: .... # OF PASSENGER SEATBELTS: ....

CAR INSURANCE COMPANY: .... POLICY #: .... EXPIRATION: ...../...../.....

DRIVING LOG:

DATE	EVENT/DESTINATION	DRIVER SIGNATURE	TROOP LEADER SIGNATURE

NAME:

☐ BACKGROUND CHECK

PHONE: (......) .... DRIVER'S LICENSE #: .... EXPIRATION: ...../...../..... LICENSE PLATE: ....

VEHICLE YEAR, MAKE & MODEL: .... # OF PASSENGER SEATBELTS: ....

CAR INSURANCE COMPANY: .... POLICY #: .... EXPIRATION: ...../...../.....

DRIVING LOG:

DATE	EVENT/DESTINATION	DRIVER SIGNATURE	TROOP LEADER SIGNATURE

VOLUNTEER DRIVER LOG

NAME: ☐ BACKGROUND CHECK

PHONE: (......) .... DRIVER'S LICENSE #: .... EXPIRATION: ....../....../...... LICENSE PLATE: ....

VEHICLE YEAR, MAKE & MODEL: .... # OF PASSENGER SEATBELTS: ....

CAR INSURANCE COMPANY: .... POLICY #: .... EXPIRATION: ....../....../......

DRIVING LOG:

DATE	EVENT/DESTINATION	DRIVER SIGNATURE	TROOP LEADER SIGNATURE

NAME: ☐ BACKGROUND CHECK

PHONE: (......) .... DRIVER'S LICENSE #: .... EXPIRATION: ....../....../...... LICENSE PLATE: ....

VEHICLE YEAR, MAKE & MODEL: .... # OF PASSENGER SEATBELTS: ....

CAR INSURANCE COMPANY: .... POLICY #: .... EXPIRATION: ....../....../......

DRIVING LOG:

DATE	EVENT/DESTINATION	DRIVER SIGNATURE	TROOP LEADER SIGNATURE

TAKING YOUR FIRST LEAP IS NECESSARY TO CREATE CHANGE. YOU ARE ALLOWED TO TAKE UP THOSE SPACES, AND DON'T YOU EVER LET ANYONE TELL YOU DIFFERENTLY."

CLIMATE ACTIVIST ISRA HIRSI

NAME: ☐ BACKGROUND CHECK

PHONE: (......)............ DRIVER'S LICENSE #:............... EXPIRATION: ..../..../.... LICENSE PLATE:...............

VEHICLE YEAR, MAKE & MODEL:.. # OF PASSENGER SEATBELTS:...............

CAR INSURANCE COMPANY:.................... POLICY #:.................... EXPIRATION: ..../..../....

DRIVING LOG:

DATE	EVENT/DESTINATION	DRIVER SIGNATURE	TROOP LEADER SIGNATURE

NAME: ☐ BACKGROUND CHECK

PHONE: (......)............ DRIVER'S LICENSE #:............... EXPIRATION: ..../..../.... LICENSE PLATE:...............

VEHICLE YEAR, MAKE & MODEL:.. # OF PASSENGER SEATBELTS:...............

CAR INSURANCE COMPANY:.................... POLICY #:.................... EXPIRATION: ..../..../....

DRIVING LOG:

DATE	EVENT/DESTINATION	DRIVER SIGNATURE	TROOP LEADER SIGNATURE

VOLUNTEER DRIVER LOG

NAME: _____   ☐ BACKGROUND CHECK

PHONE: (_____) .... DRIVER'S LICENSE #: .... EXPIRATION: ...../...../..... LICENSE PLATE: ....

VEHICLE YEAR, MAKE & MODEL: .... # OF PASSENGER SEATBELTS: ....

CAR INSURANCE COMPANY: .... POLICY #: .... EXPIRATION: ...../...../.....

DRIVING LOG:

DATE	EVENT/DESTINATION	DRIVER SIGNATURE	TROOP LEADER SIGNATURE

NAME: _____   ☐ BACKGROUND CHECK

PHONE: (_____) .... DRIVER'S LICENSE #: .... EXPIRATION: ...../...../..... LICENSE PLATE: ....

VEHICLE YEAR, MAKE & MODEL: .... # OF PASSENGER SEATBELTS: ....

CAR INSURANCE COMPANY: .... POLICY #: .... EXPIRATION: ...../...../.....

DRIVING LOG:

DATE	EVENT/DESTINATION	DRIVER SIGNATURE	TROOP LEADER SIGNATURE

Made in the USA
Monee, IL
18 November 2023

46847065R00083